My brain is a bad guy brain.

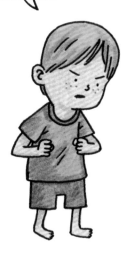

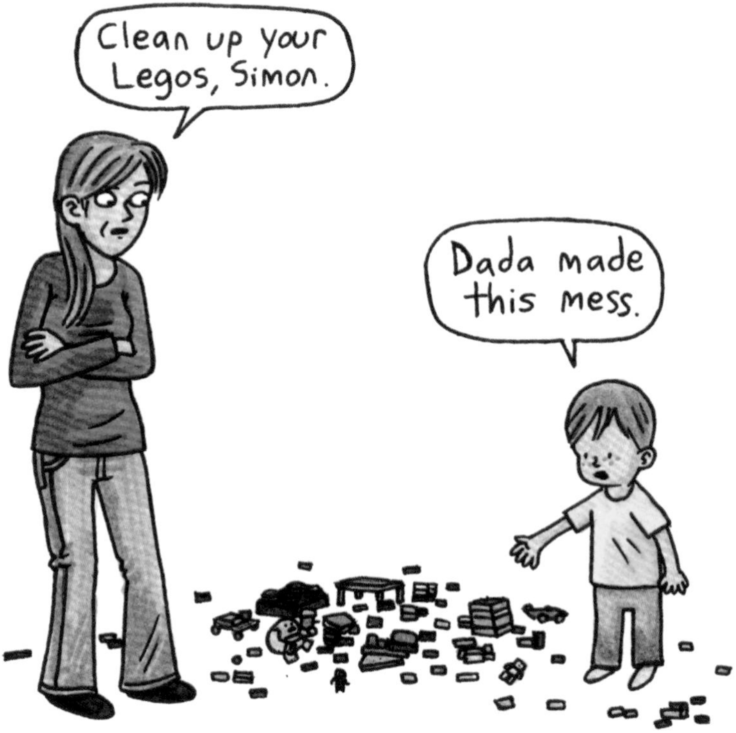
Clean up your Legos, Simon.
Dada made this mess.

KIDS ARE STILL WEIRD

And More Observations from Parenthood

BY
JEFFREY BROWN

Thank you to J.T. Yost and everyone at NBM, Marc Gerald, Izzy, Lawrence, Ewelina, and all my friends and family, especially Jennifer, Oscar, and Simon.

Original *Kids Are Weird* book design by Michael Morris

ISBN 9781681123448

Library of Congress Control Number: 9781681123448
Printed in China
First printing October 2024

This book is also available in e-book format (ISBN 9781681123455)

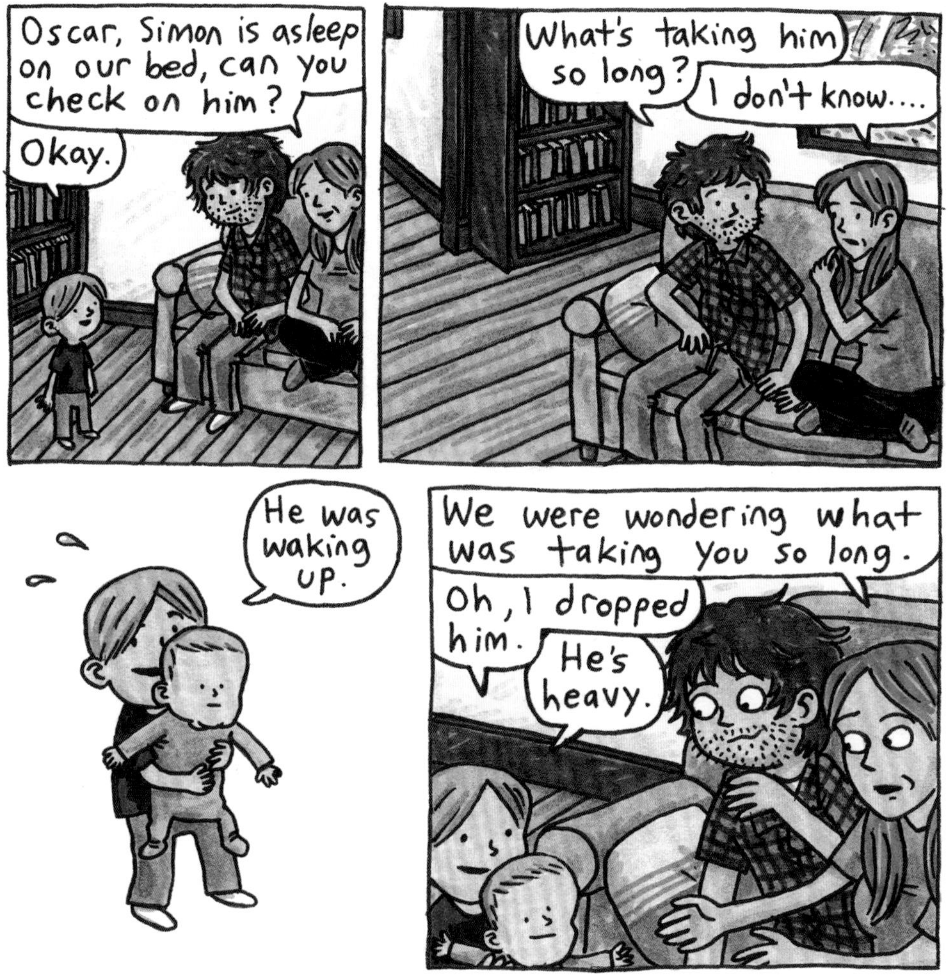
Oscar, Simon is asleep on our bed, can you check on him?
Okay.
What's taking him so long?
I don't know....
He was waking up.
We were wondering what was taking you so long.
Oh, I dropped him.
He's heavy.

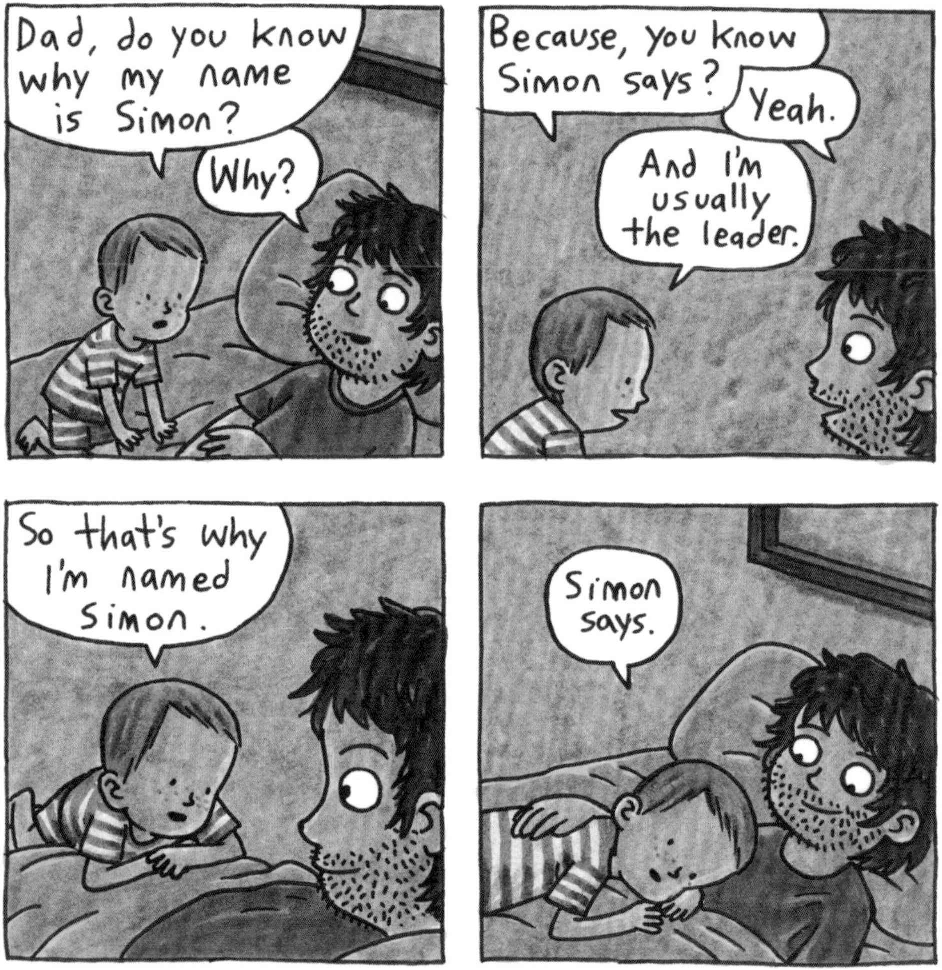
Dad, do you know why my name is Simon?
Why?
Because, you know Simon says?
Yeah.
And I'm usually the leader.
So that's why I'm named Simon.
Simon says.

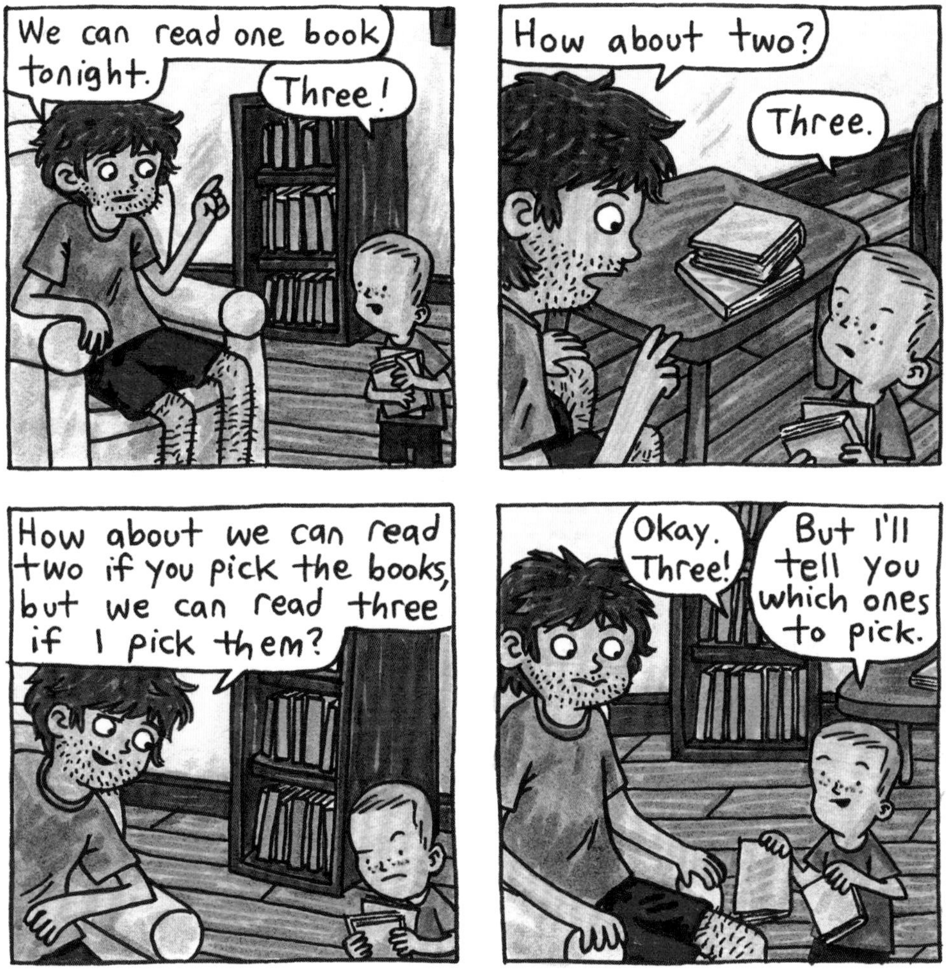
We can read one book tonight.
Three!
How about two?
Three.
How about we can read two if you pick the books, but we can read three if I pick them?
Okay. Three!
But I'll tell you which ones to pick.

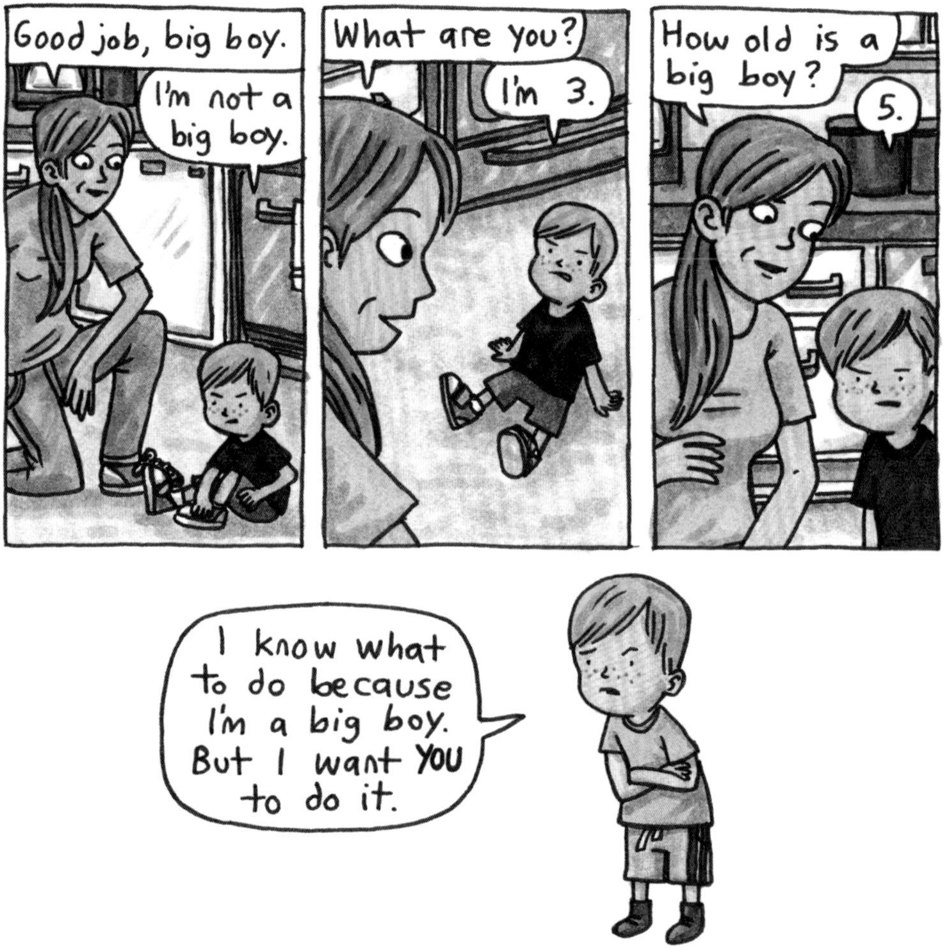
Good job, big boy.
I'm not a big boy.
What are you?
I'm 3.
How old is a big boy?
5.
I know what to do because I'm a big boy. But I want YOU to do it.

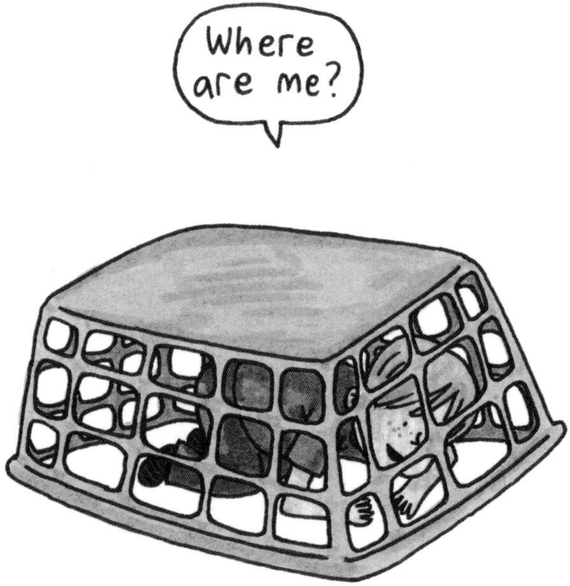
Where are me?

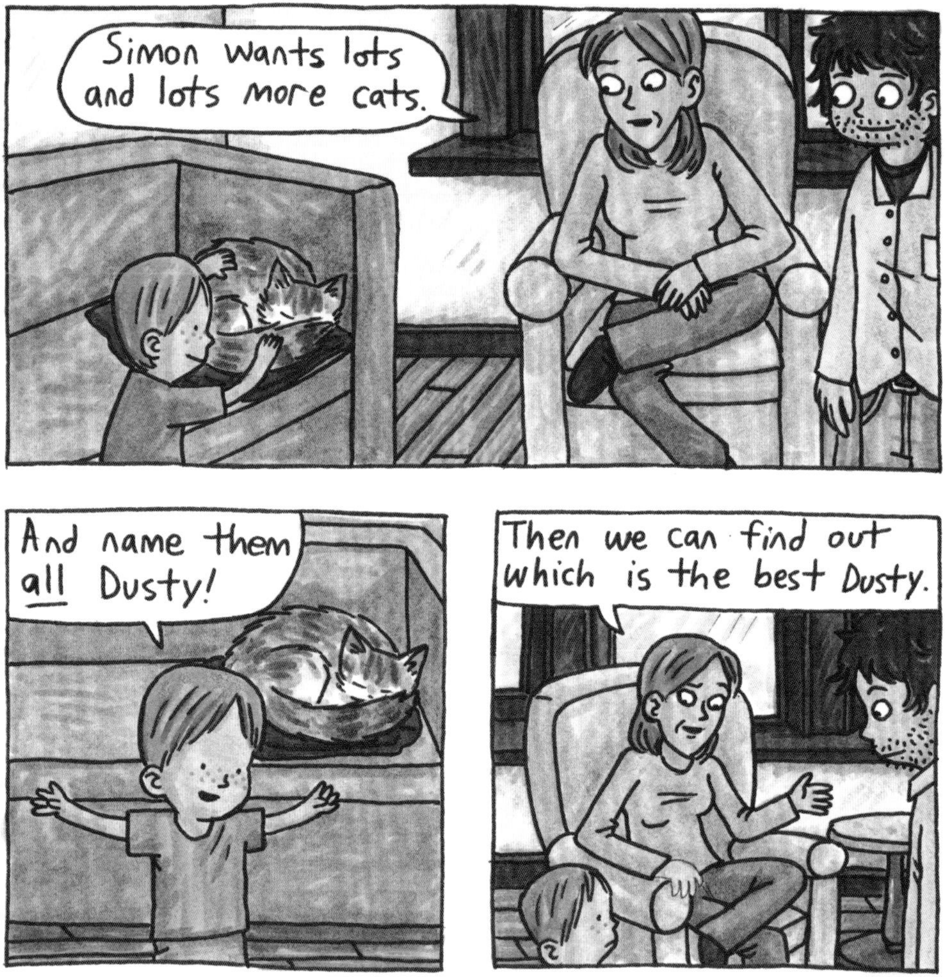
Simon wants lots and lots more cats.
And name them all Dusty!
Then we can find out which is the best Dusty.

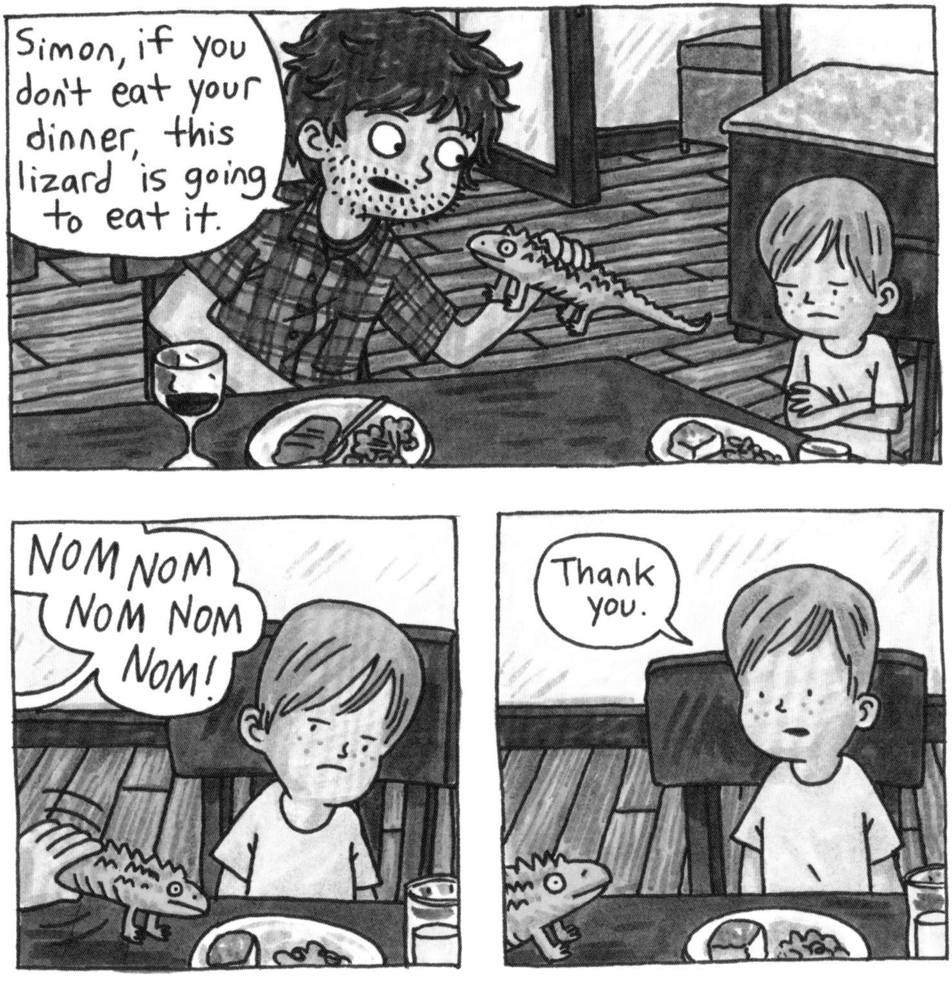
Simon, if you don't eat your dinner, this lizard is going to eat it.
NOM NOM NOM NOM NOM!
Thank you.

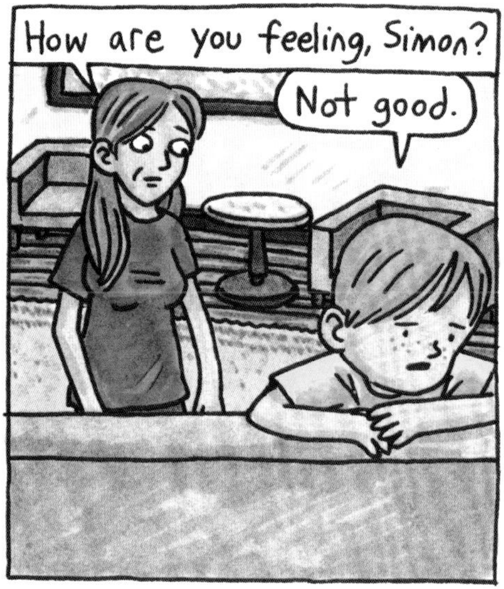
How are you feeling, Simon?
Not good.

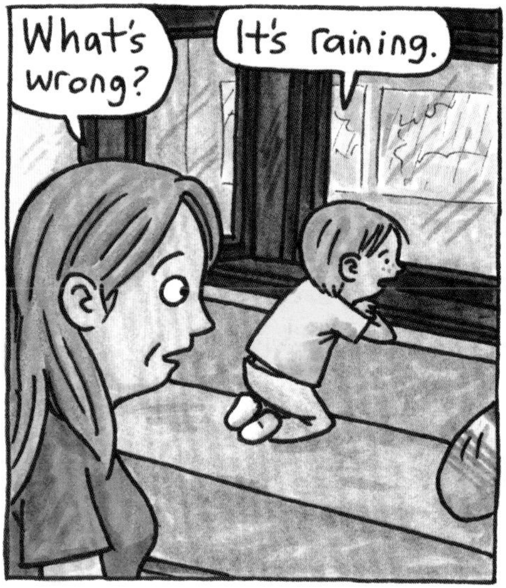
What's wrong?
It's raining.

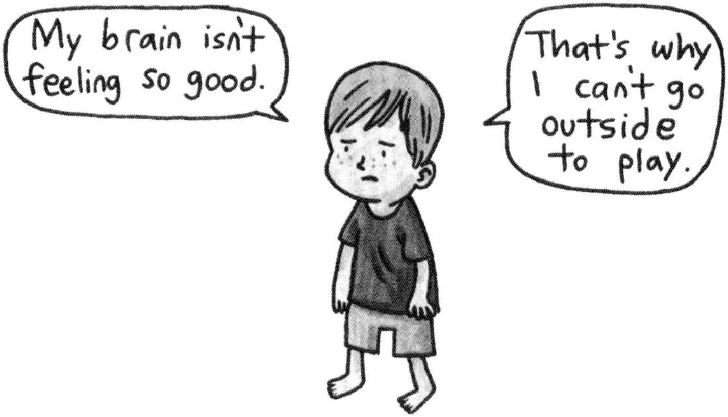
My brain isn't feeling so good.
That's why I can't go outside to play.

Who's YOUR greatest enemy, Daddy?
I don't know... I don't think I really have a greatest enemy.
BATMAN
I know who your greatest enemy is.
It's yourself.

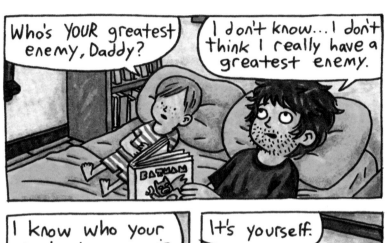

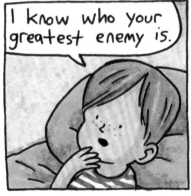

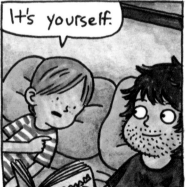

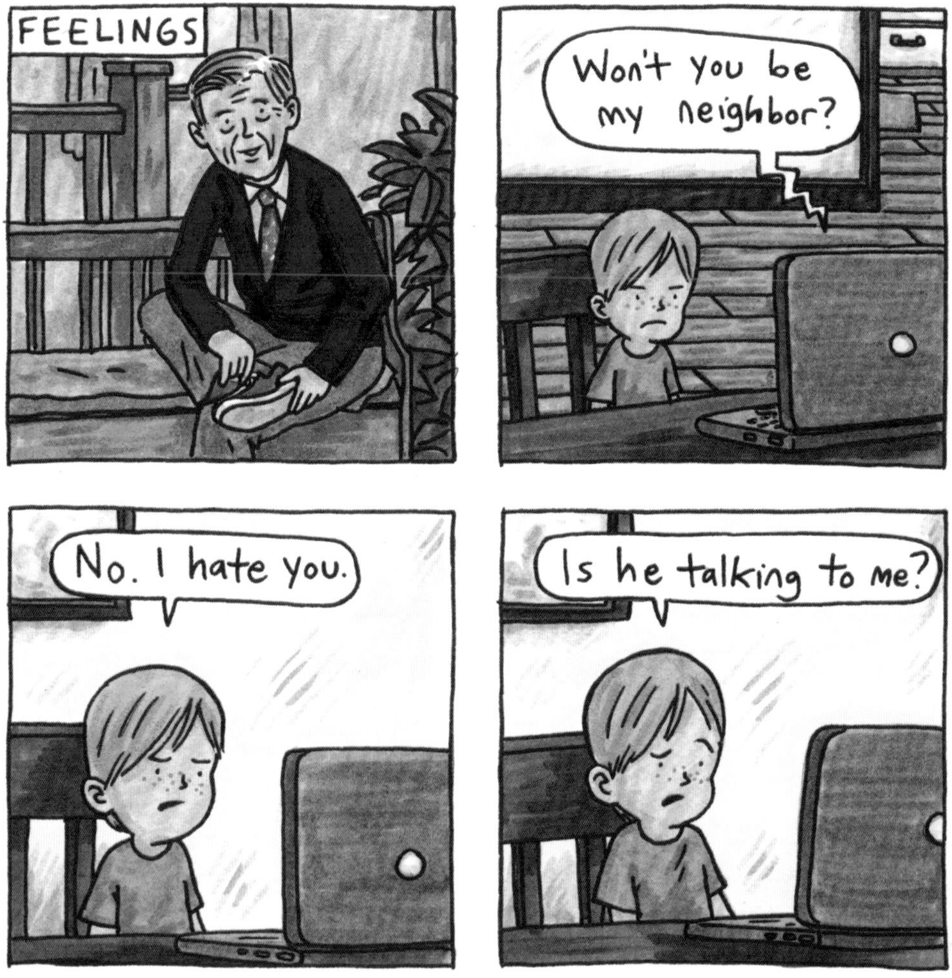
FEELINGS
Won't you be my neighbor?
No. I hate you.
Is he talking to me?

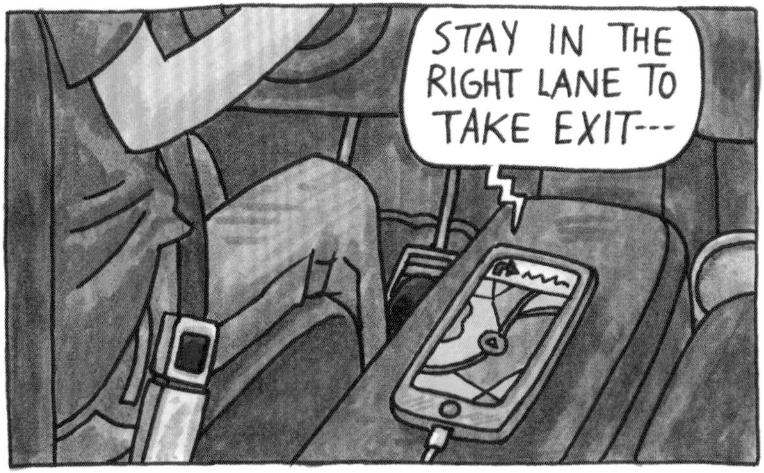
STAY IN THE RIGHT LANE TO TAKE EXIT---

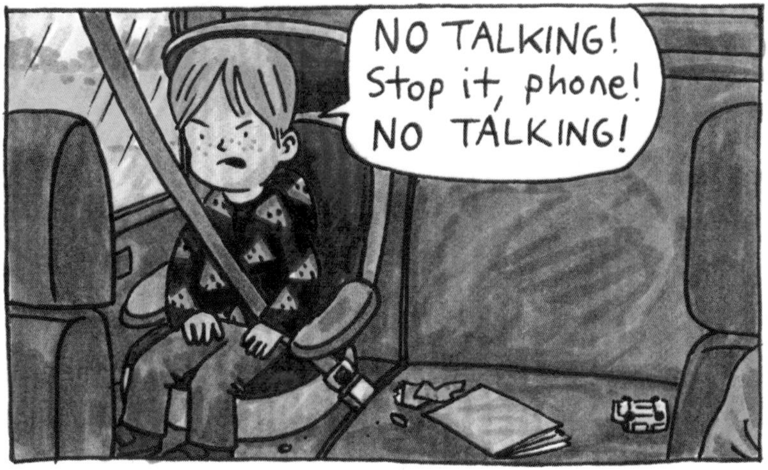
NO TALKING! Stop it, phone! NO TALKING!

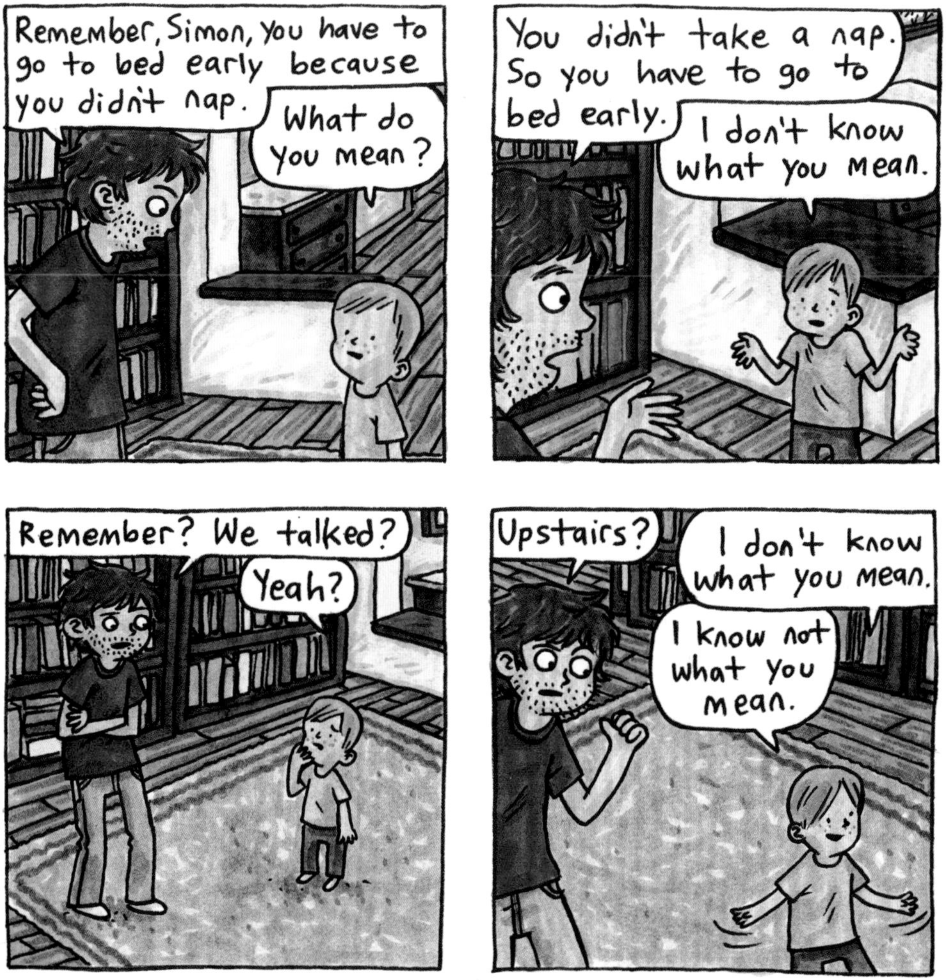
Remember, Simon, you have to go to bed early because you didn't nap.
What do you mean?
You didn't take a nap. So you have to go to bed early.
I don't know what you mean.
Remember? We talked?
Yeah?
Upstairs?
I don't know what you mean.
I know not what you mean.

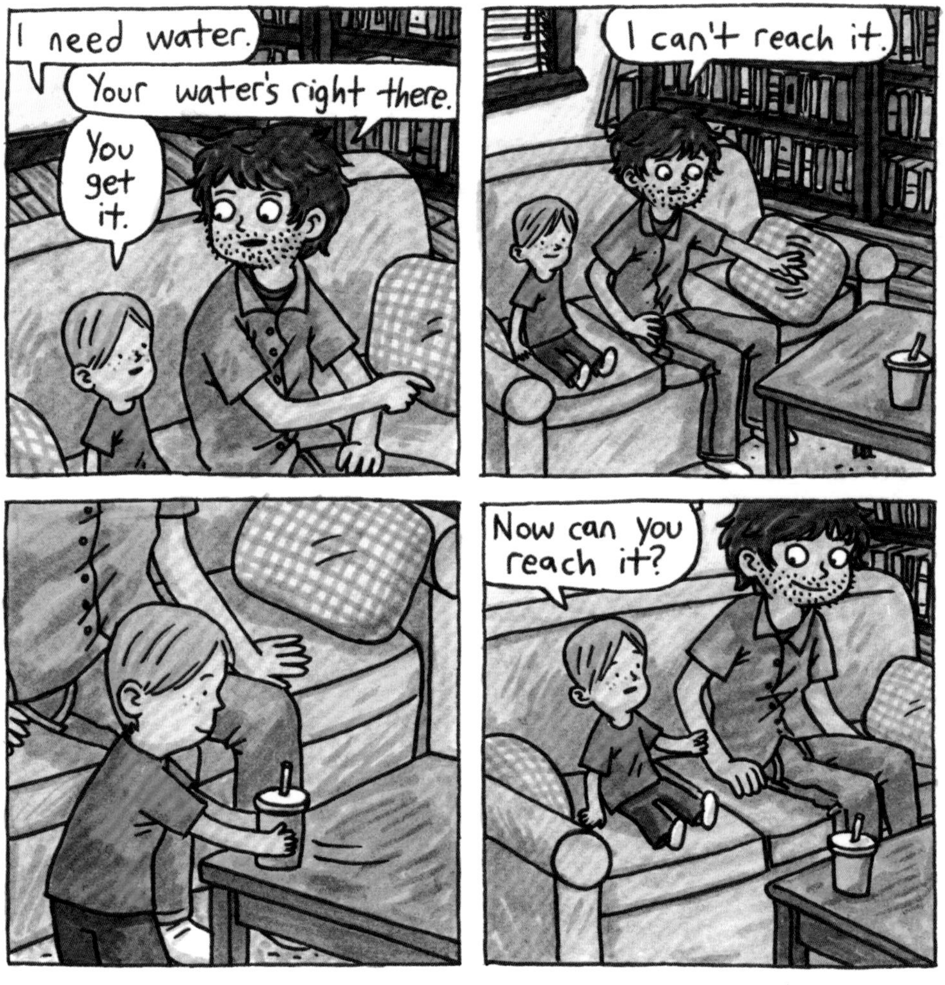
I need water.
Your water's right there.
You get it.
I can't reach it.
Now can you reach it?

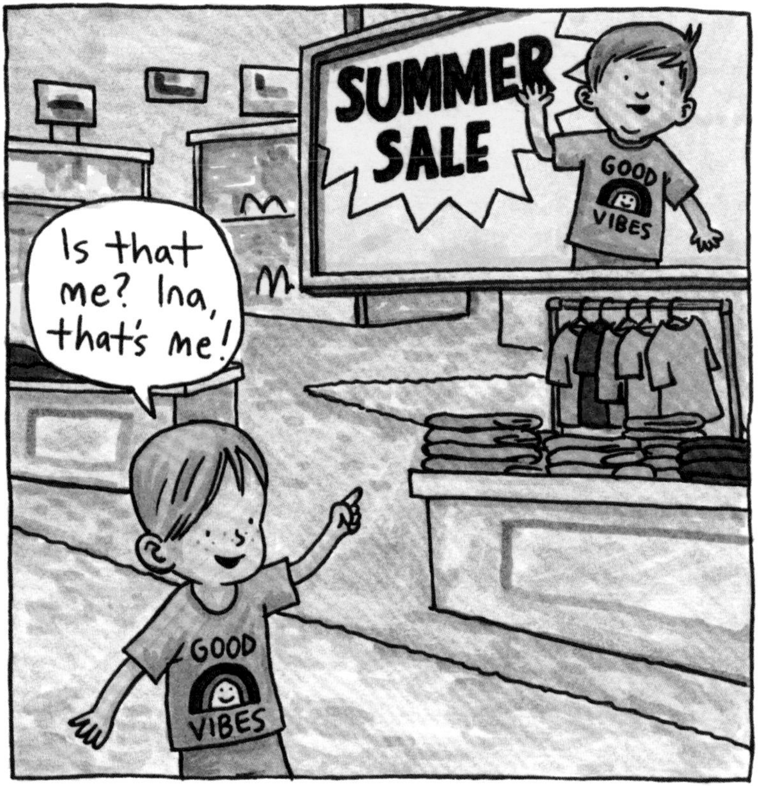
SUMMER SALE
GOOD VIBES
Is that me? Ina, that's me!
GOOD VIBES

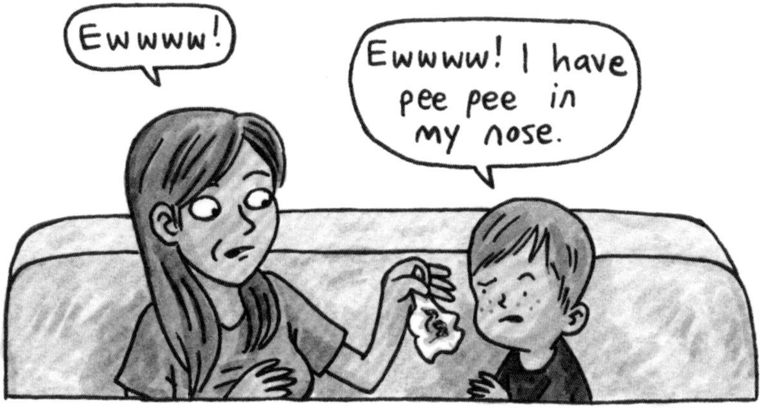
Ewwww!
Ewwww! I have pee pee in my nose.

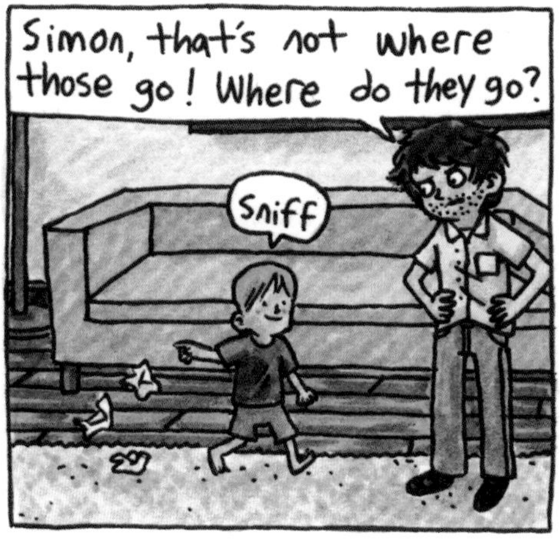
Simon, that's not where those go! Where do they go?
Sniff

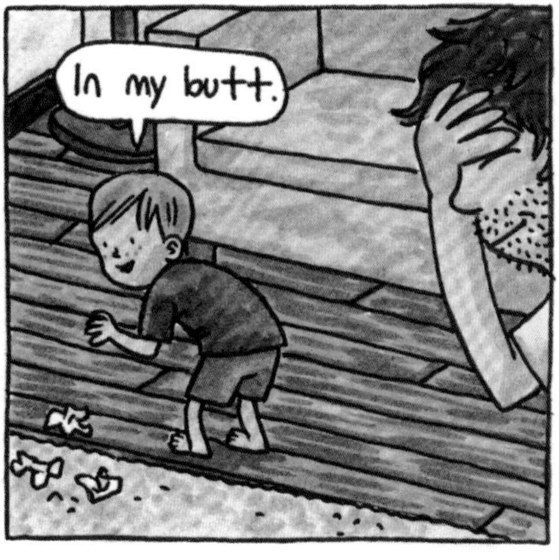
In my butt.

Wanhh! Wanhh!
No.
I'm waiting for Dada.

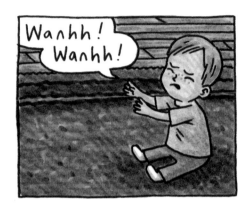

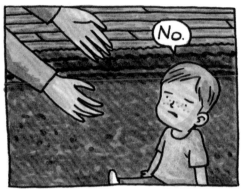

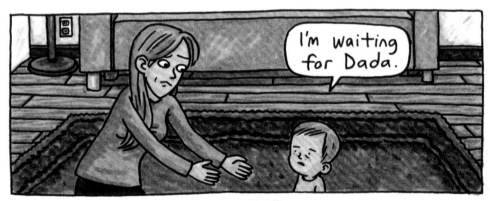

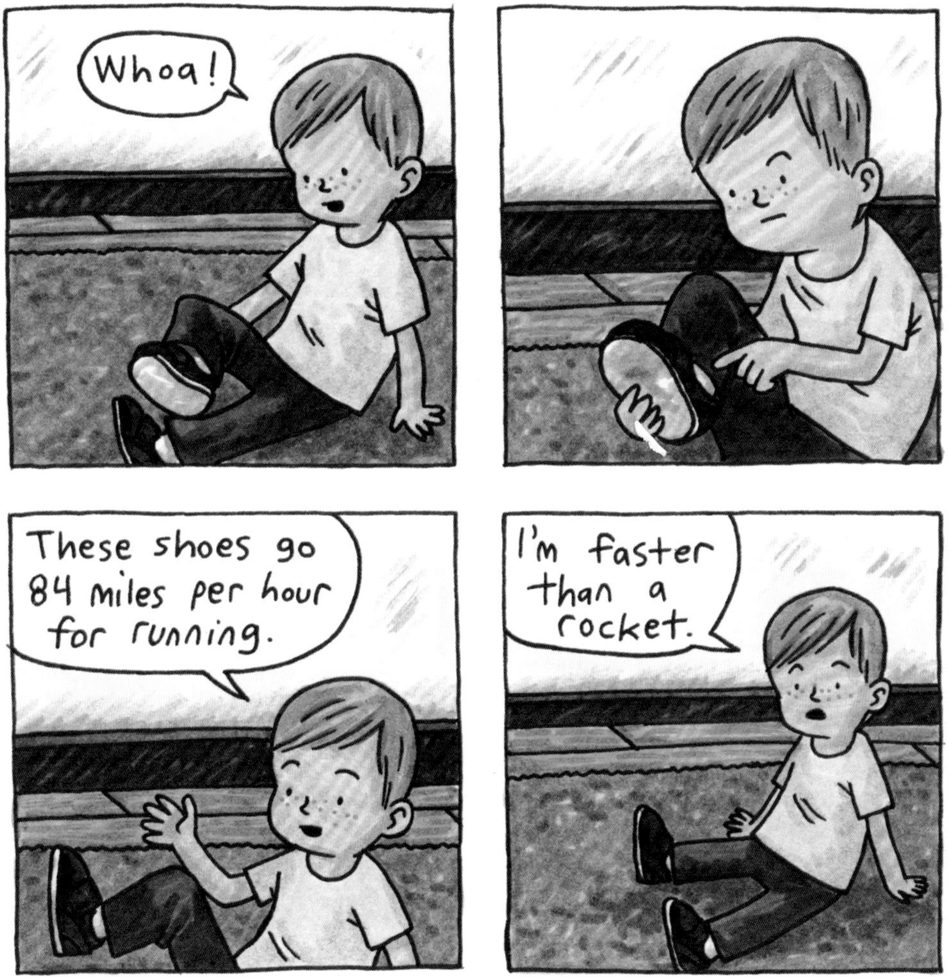
Whoa!
These shoes go 84 miles per hour for running.
I'm faster than a rocket.

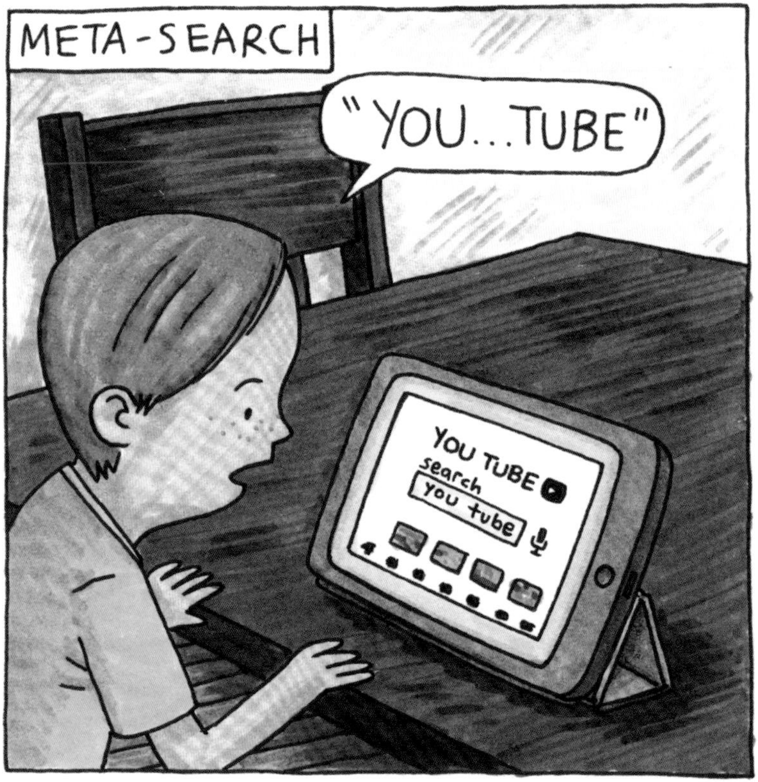
META-SEARCH
"YOU...TUBE"
YOU TUBE
search
you tube

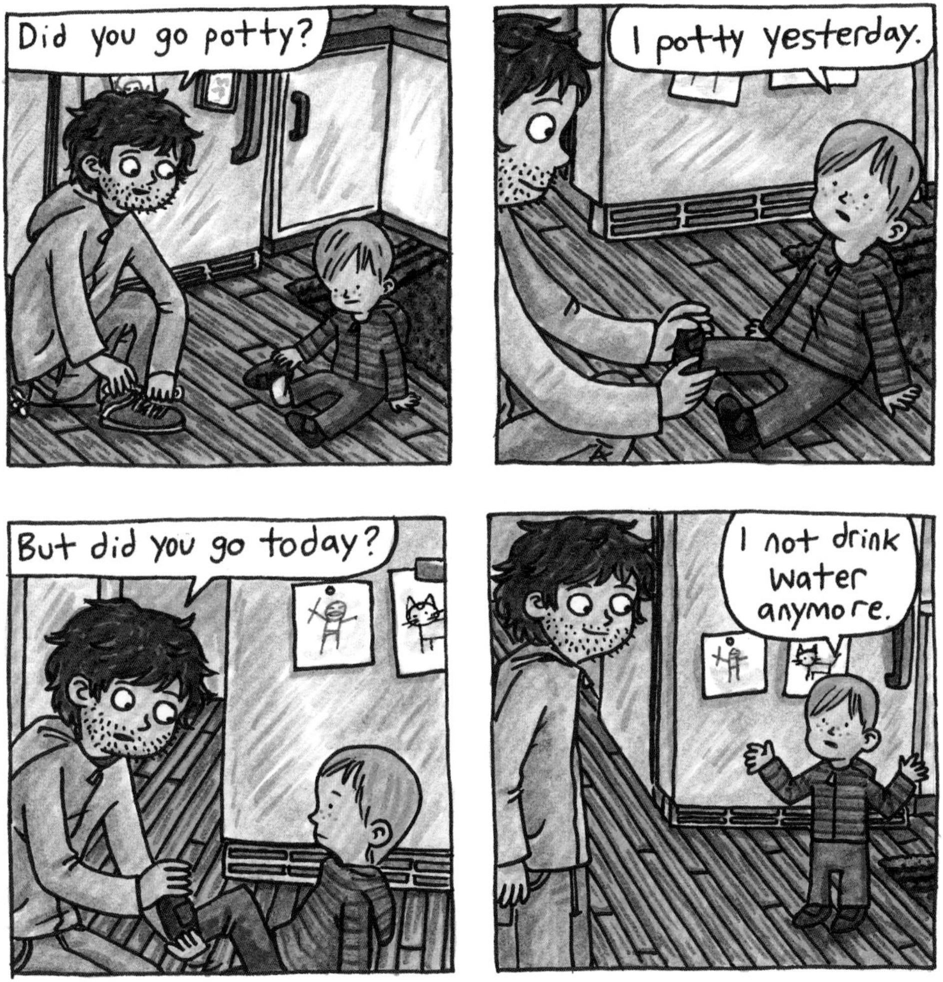
Did you go potty?
I potty yesterday.
But did you go today?
I not drink water anymore.

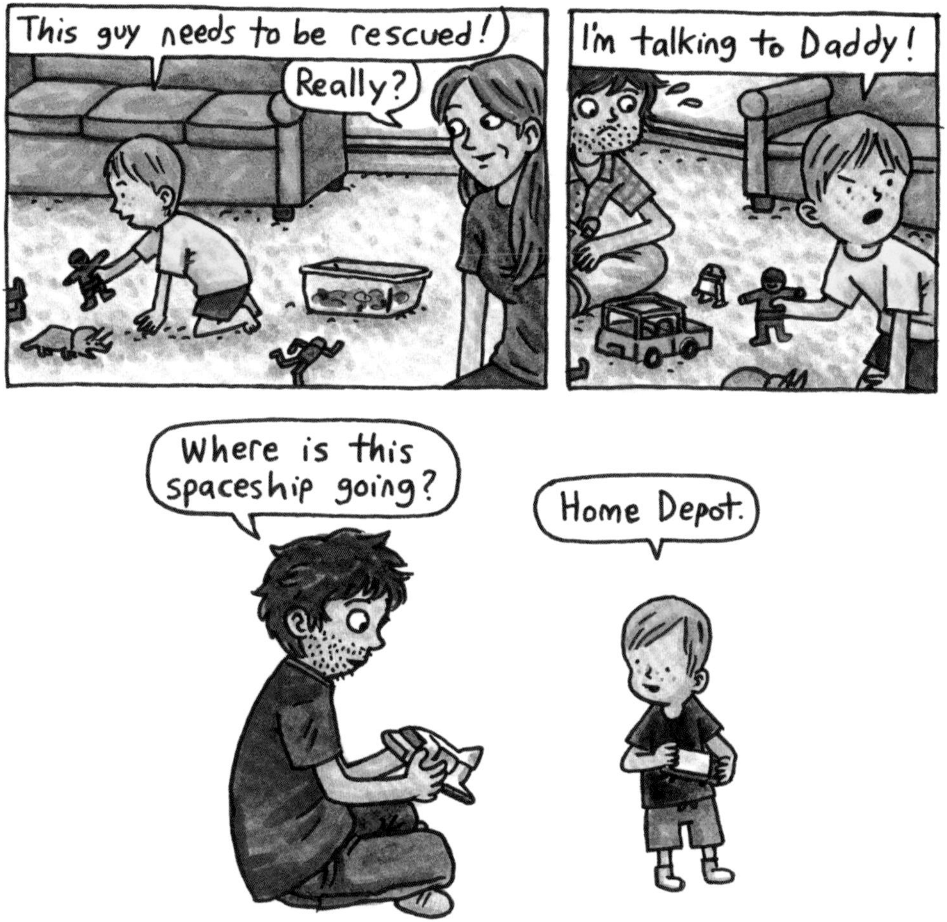
This guy needs to be rescued!
Really?
I'm talking to Daddy!
Where is this spaceship going?
Home Depot.

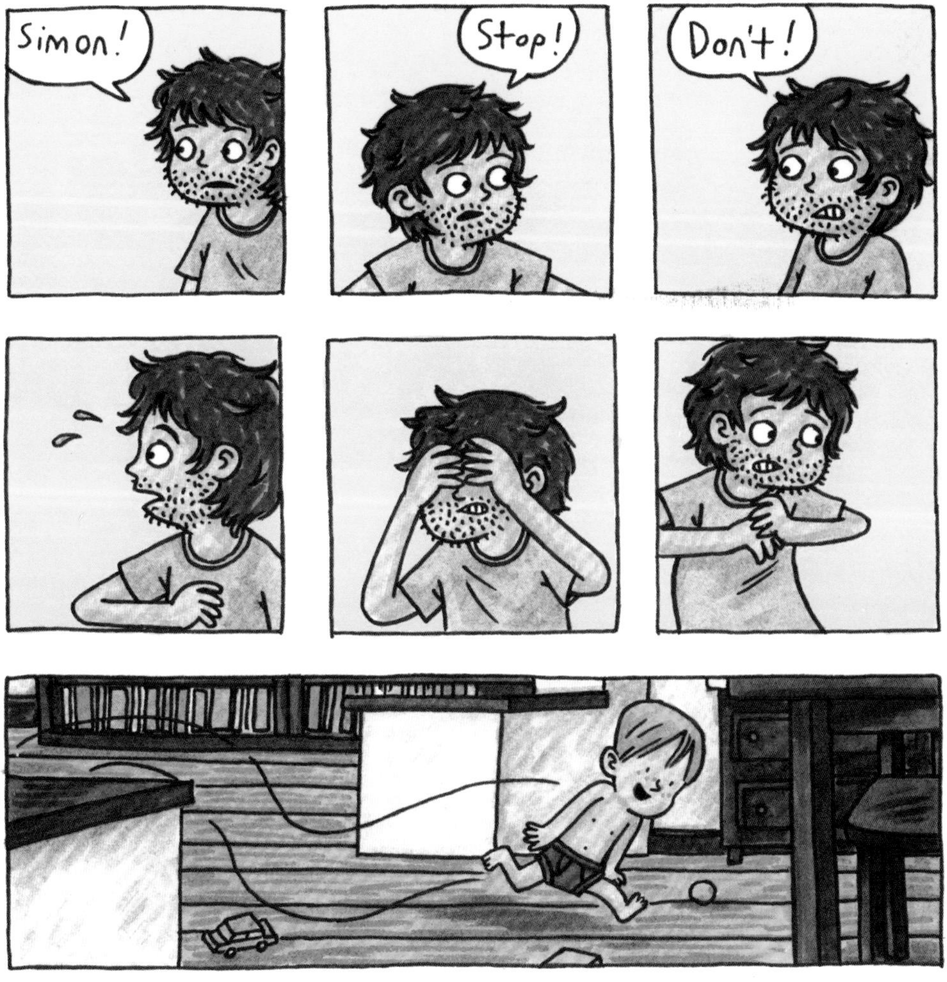
Simon!
Stop!
Don't!

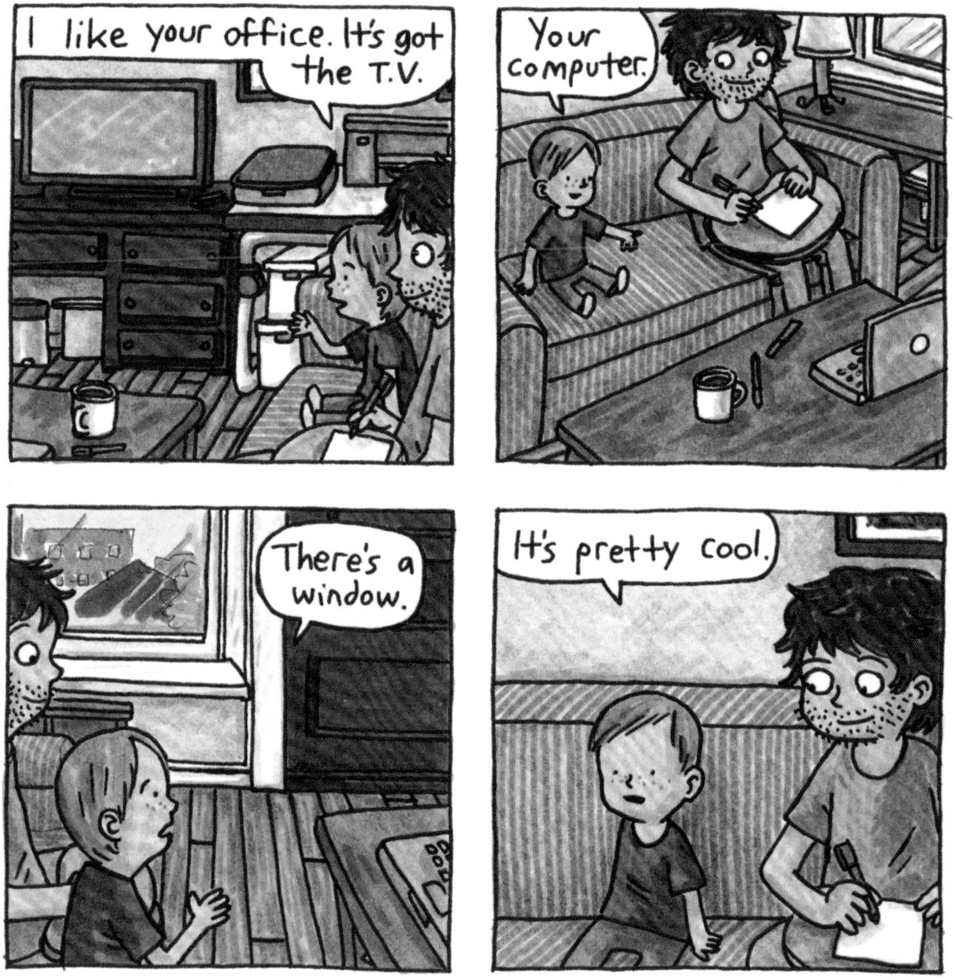
I like your office. It's got the T.V.
Your computer.
There's a window.
It's pretty cool.

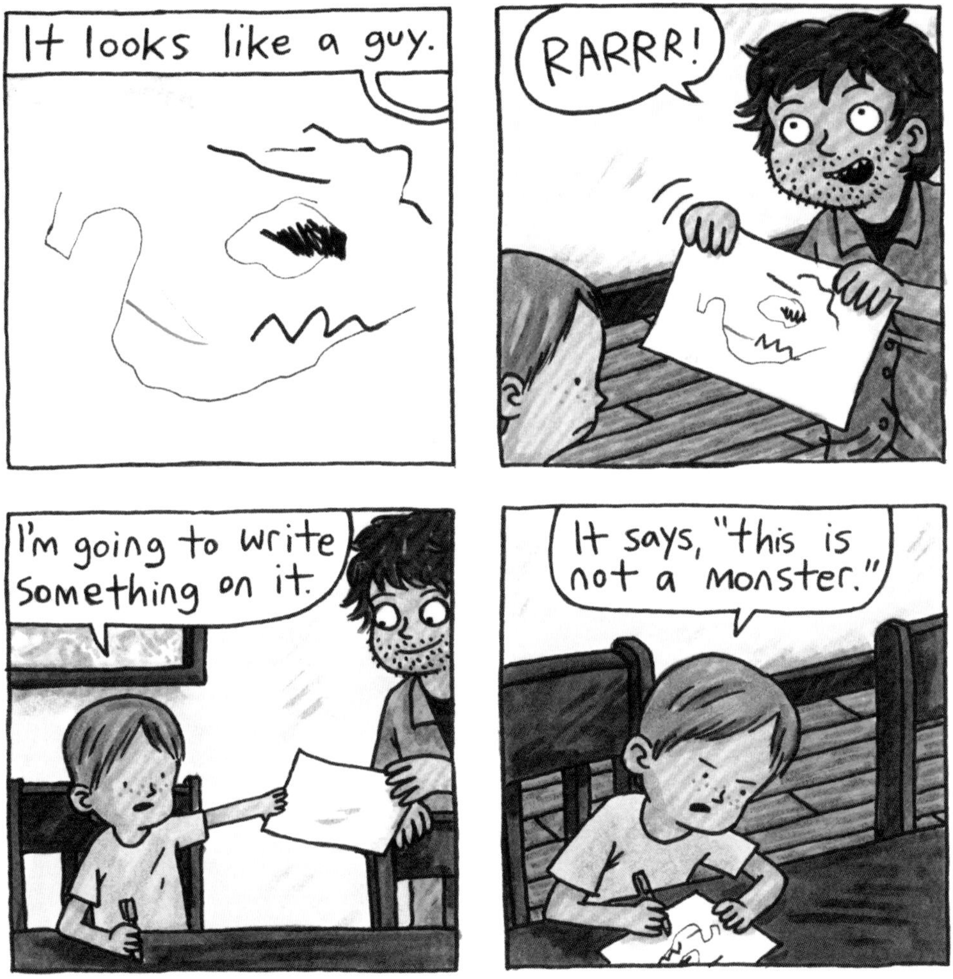
It looks like a guy.
RARRR!
I'm going to write something on it.
It says, "this is not a monster."

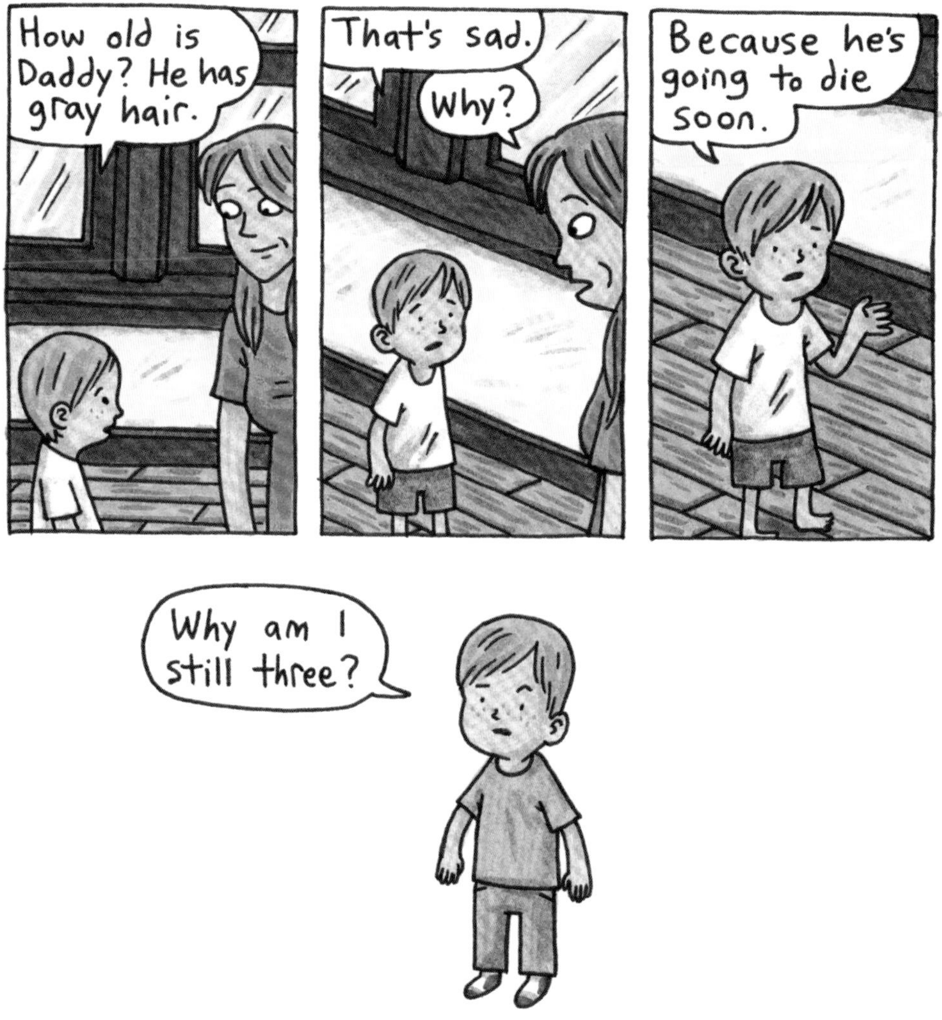
How old is Daddy? He has gray hair.
That's sad.
Why?
Because he's going to die soon.
Why am I still three?

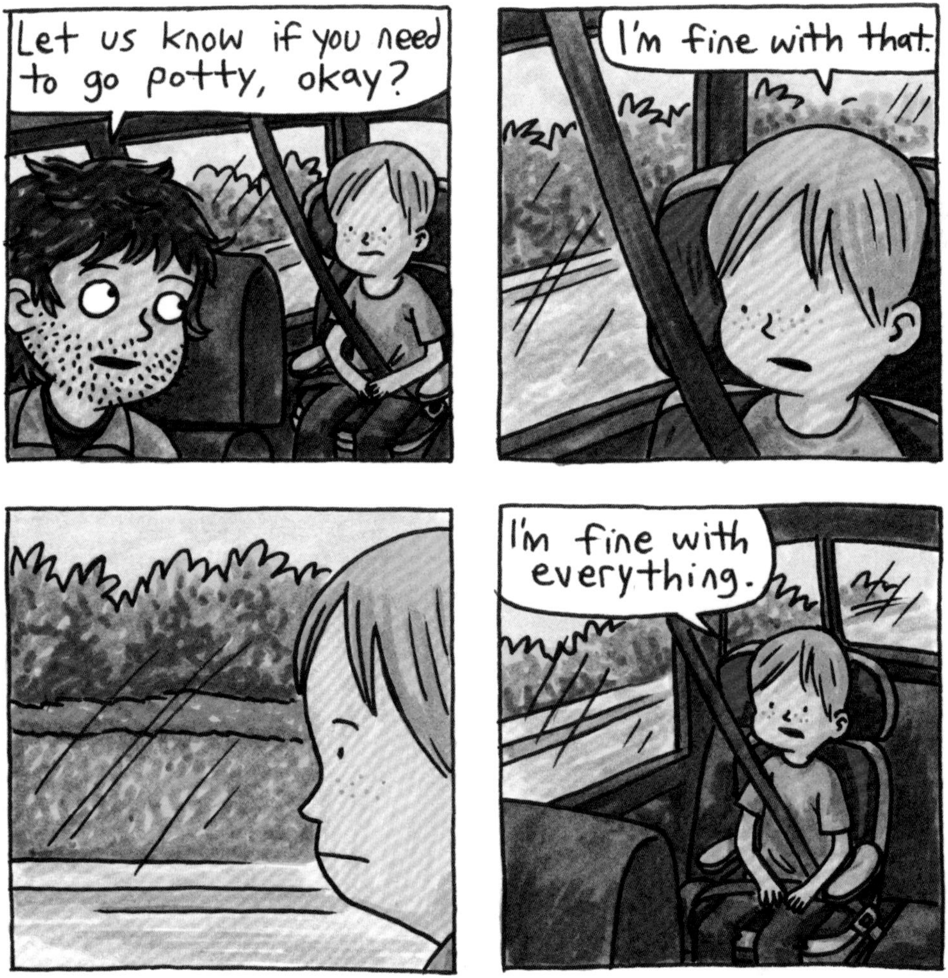
Let us know if you need to go potty, okay?
I'm fine with that.
I'm fine with everything.

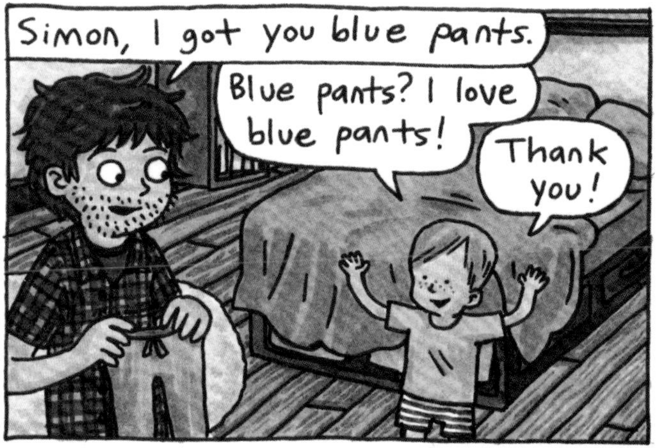
Simon, I got you blue pants.
Blue pants? I love blue pants!
Thank you!

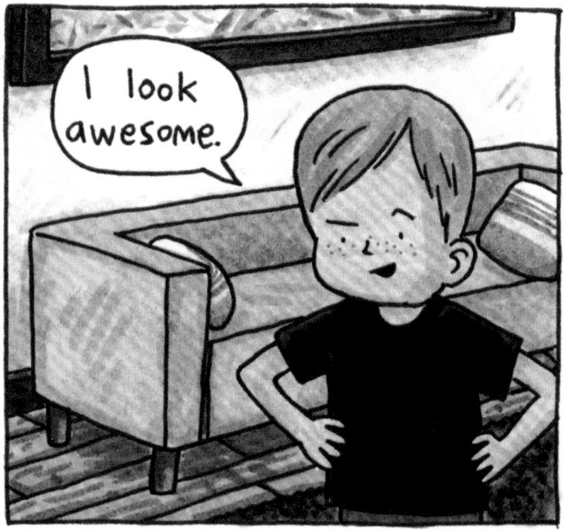
I look awesome.

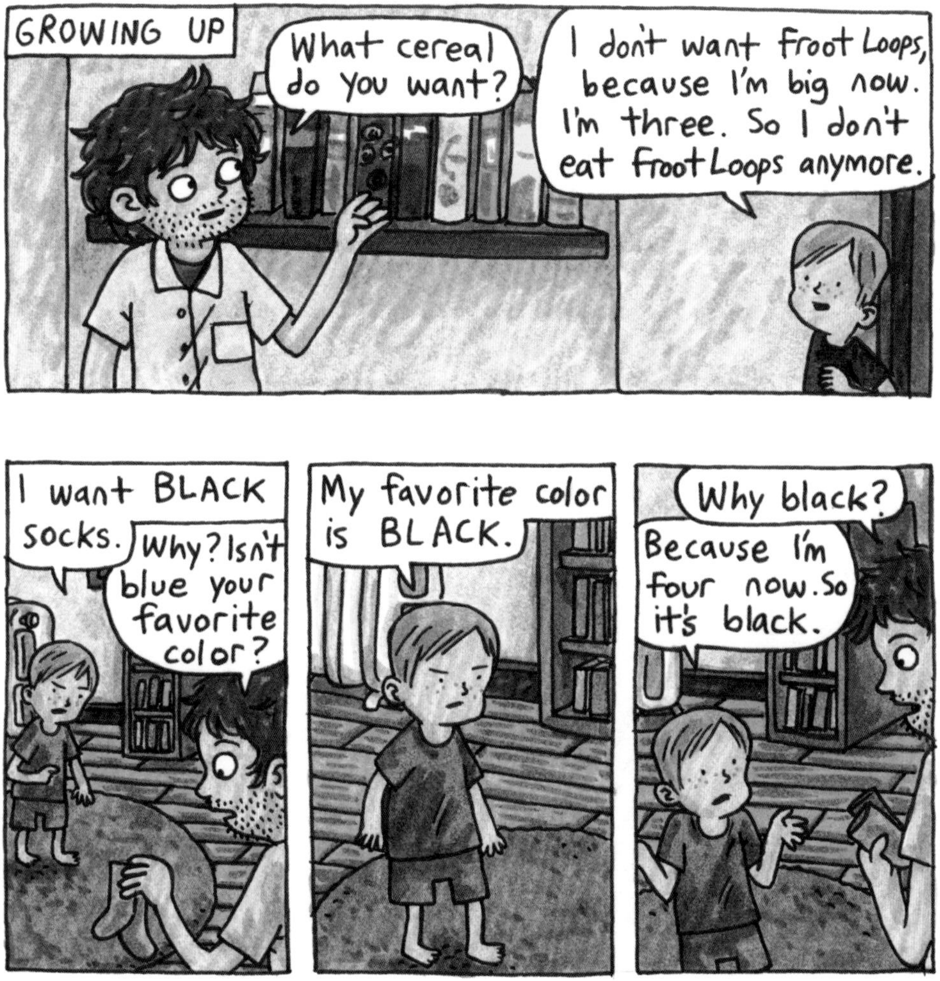
GROWING UP
What cereal do you want?
I don't want Froot Loops, because I'm big now. I'm three. So I don't eat Froot Loops anymore.
I want BLACK socks.
Why? Isn't blue your favorite color?
My favorite color is BLACK.
Why black?
Because I'm four now. So it's black.

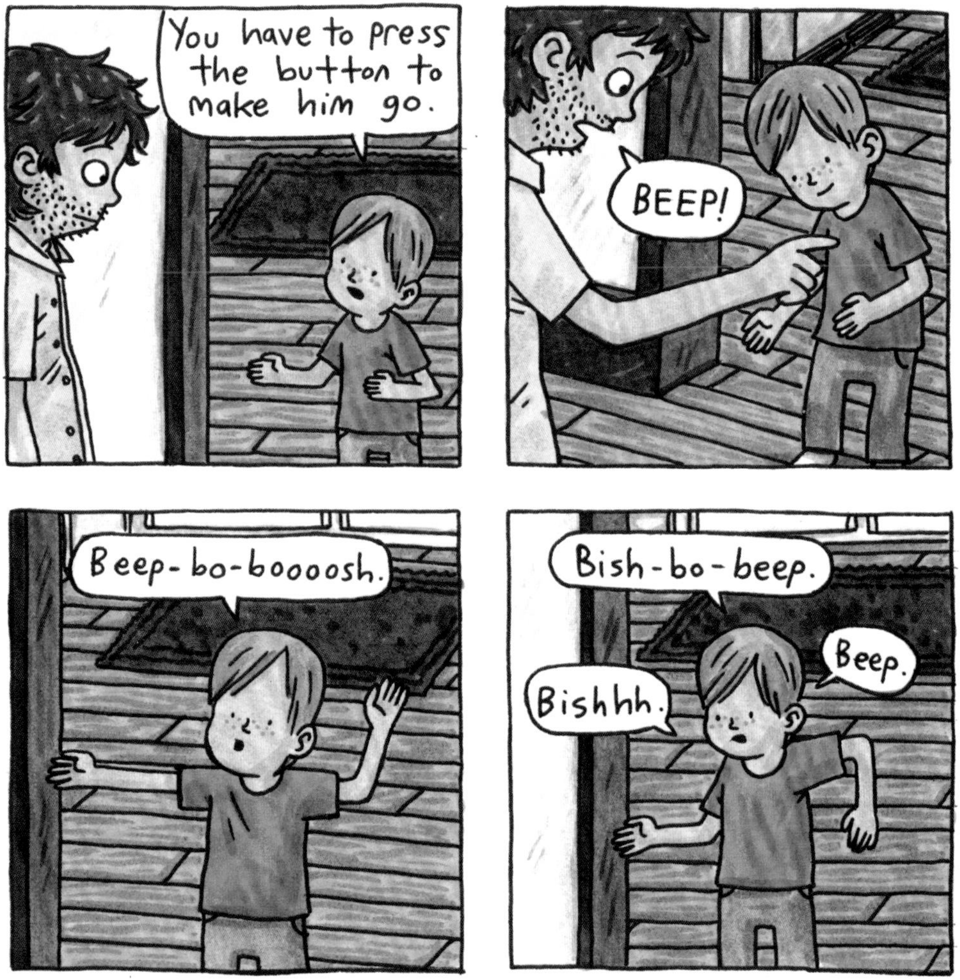
You have to press the button to make him go.
BEEP!
Beep-bo-boooosh.
Bish-bo-beep.
Bishhh.
Beep.

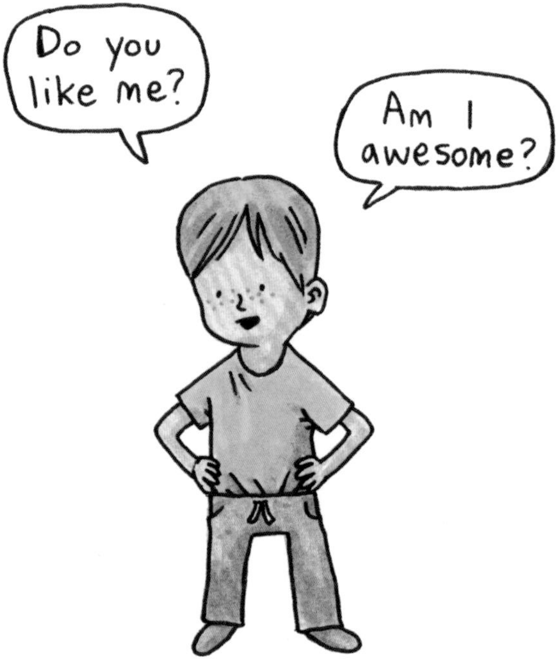
Do you like me?
Am I awesome?

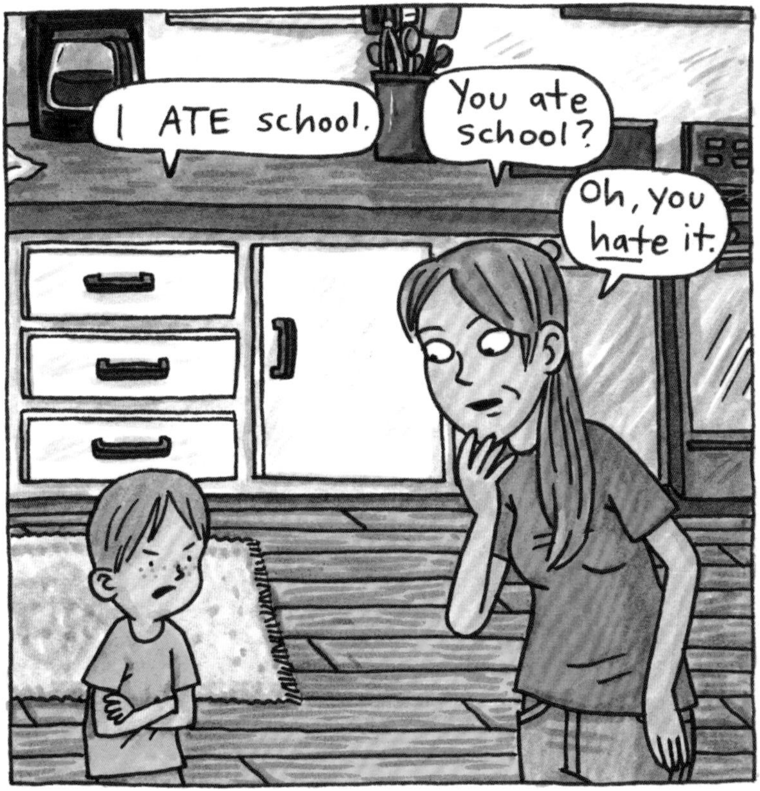
I ATE school.
You ate school?
Oh, you hate it.

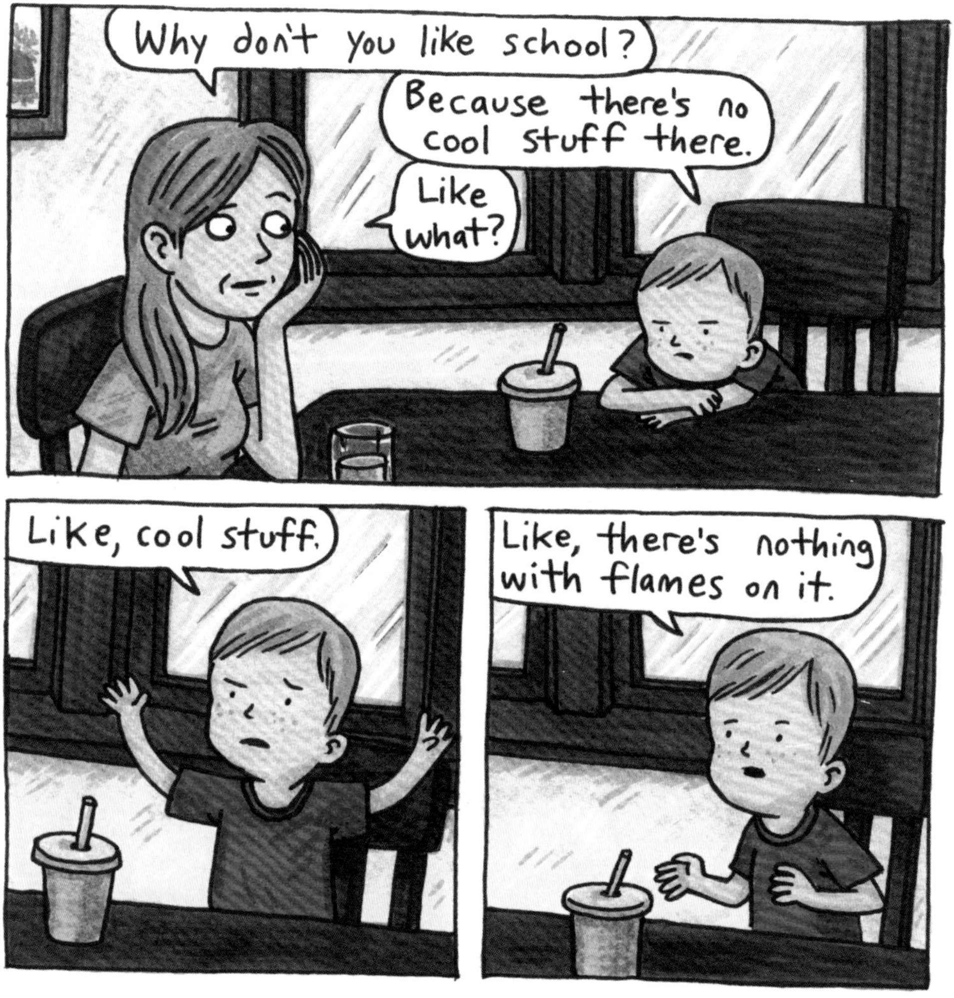
Why don't you like school?
Because there's no cool stuff there.
Like what?
Like, cool stuff.
Like, there's nothing with flames on it.

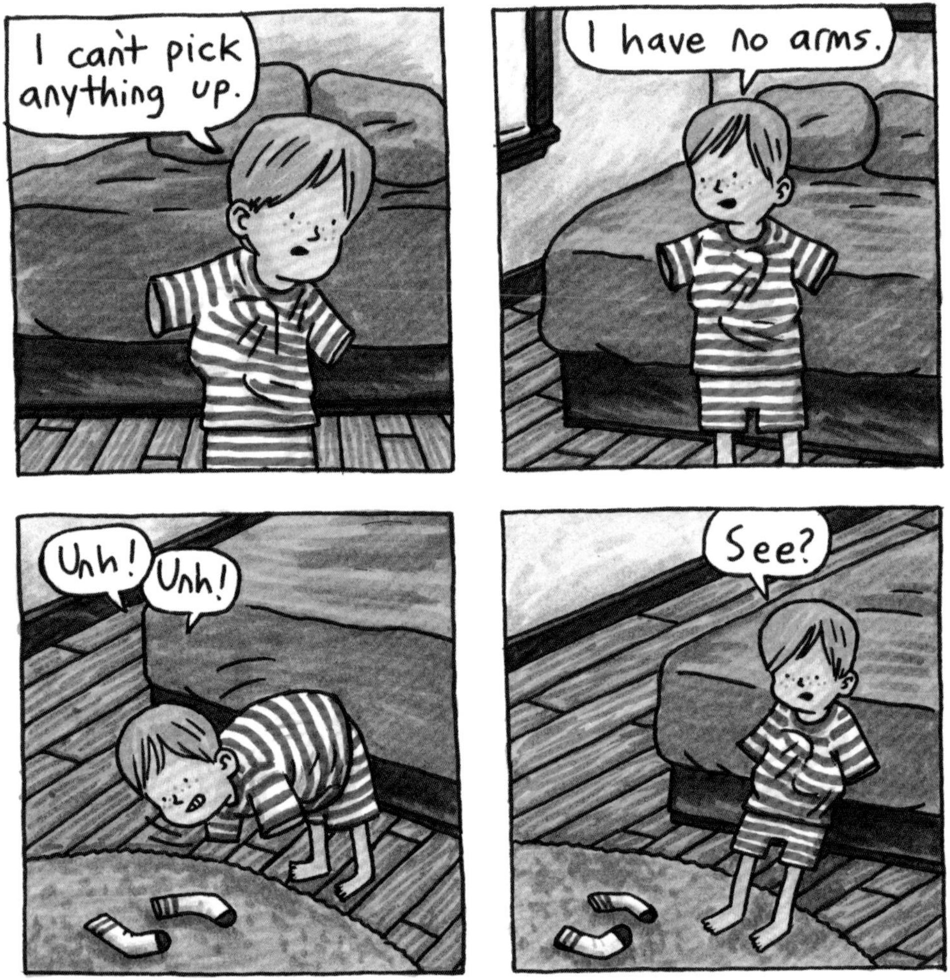
I can't pick anything up.
I have no arms.
Unh!
Unh!
See?

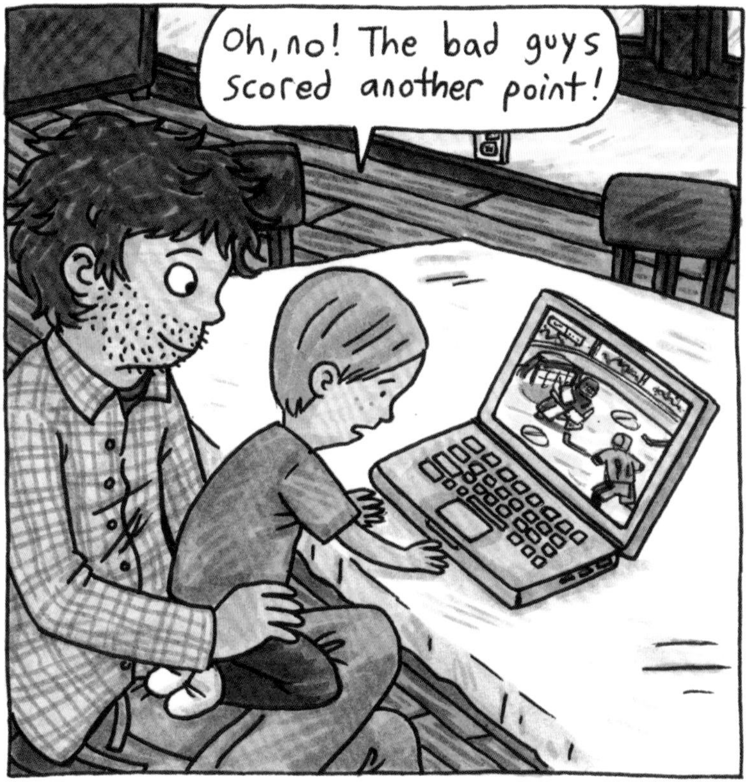
Oh, no! The bad guys scored another point!

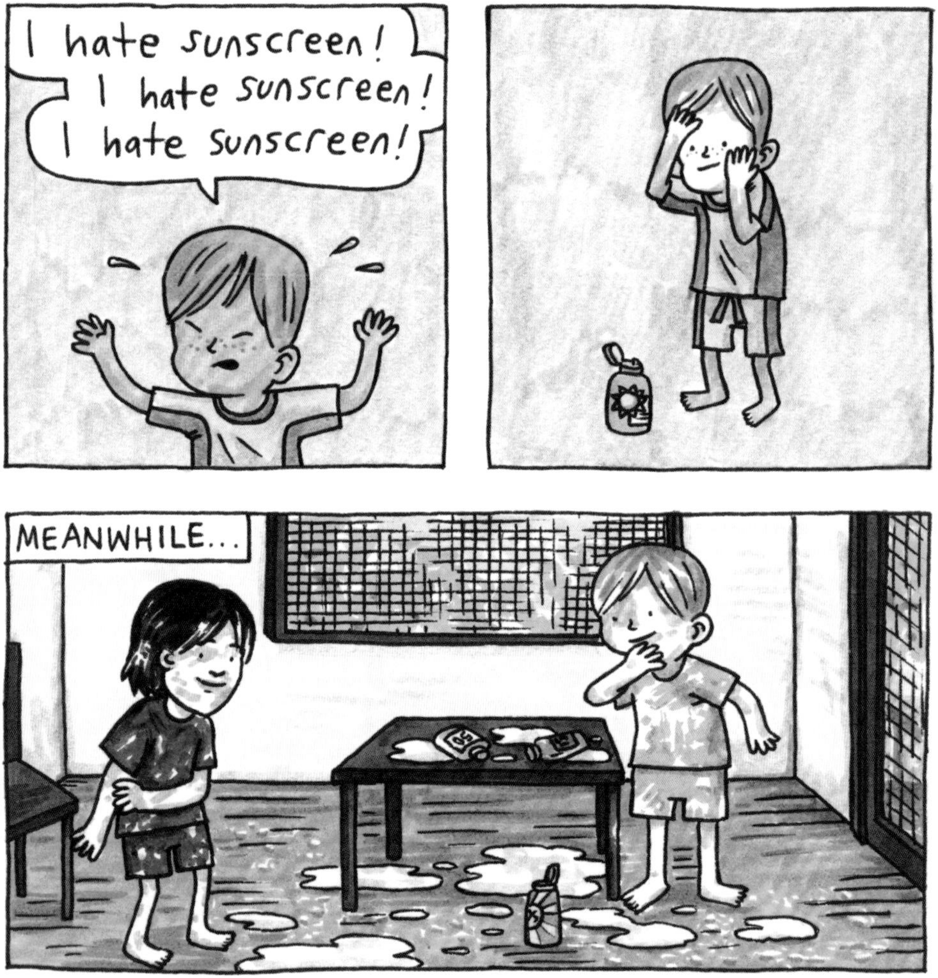
I hate sunscreen! I hate sunscreen! I hate sunscreen!
MEANWHILE...

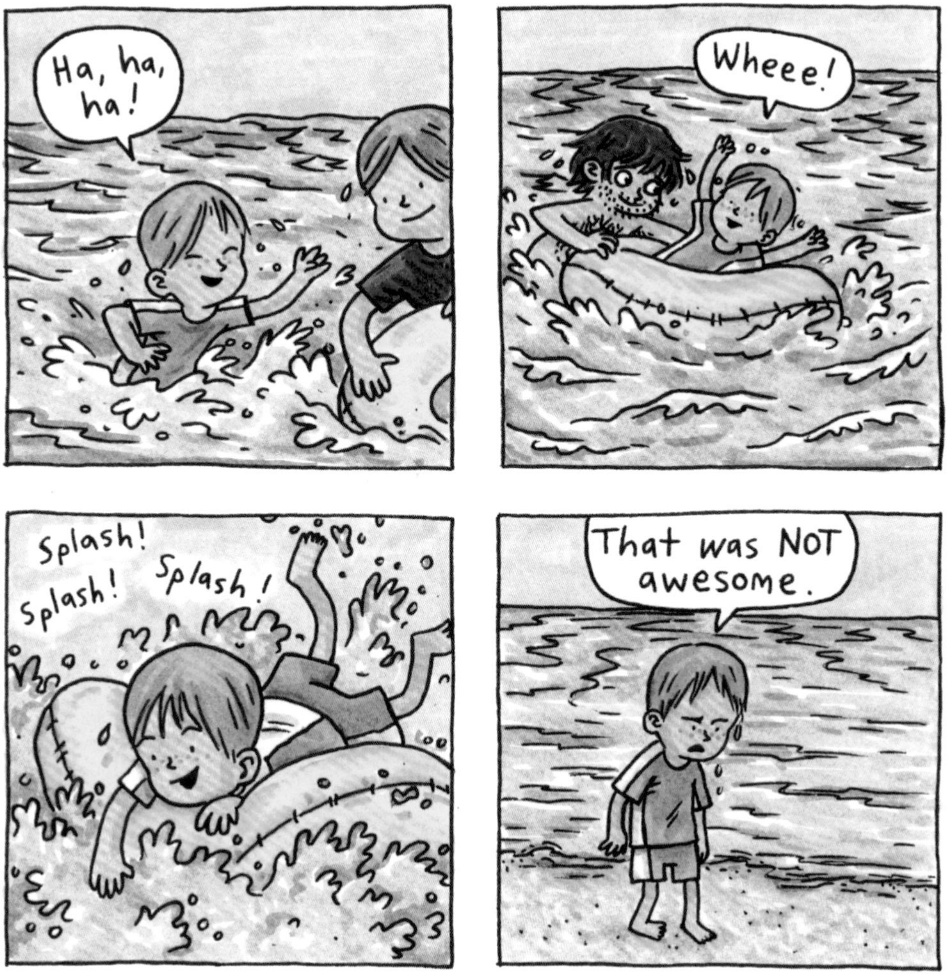
Ha, ha, ha!
Wheee!
Splash!
Splash!
Splash!
That was NOT awesome.

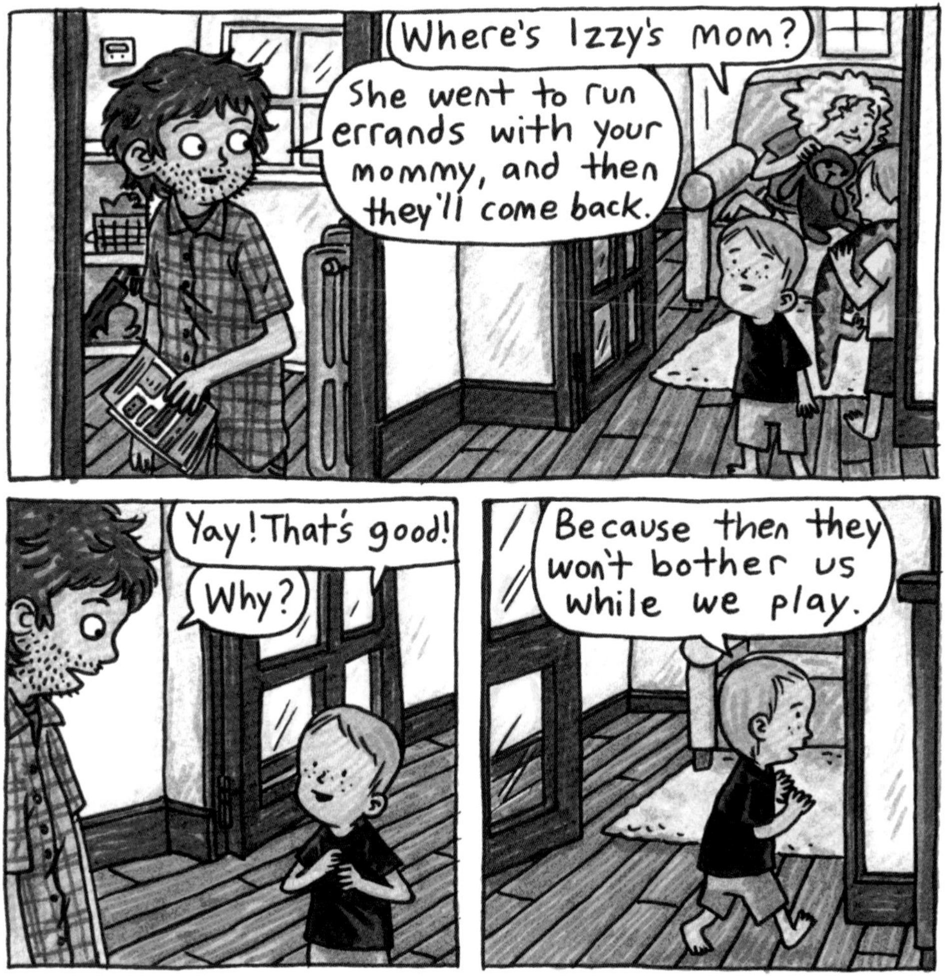
Where's Izzy's mom?
She went to run errands with your mommy, and then they'll come back.
Yay! That's good!
Why?
Because then they won't bother us while we play.

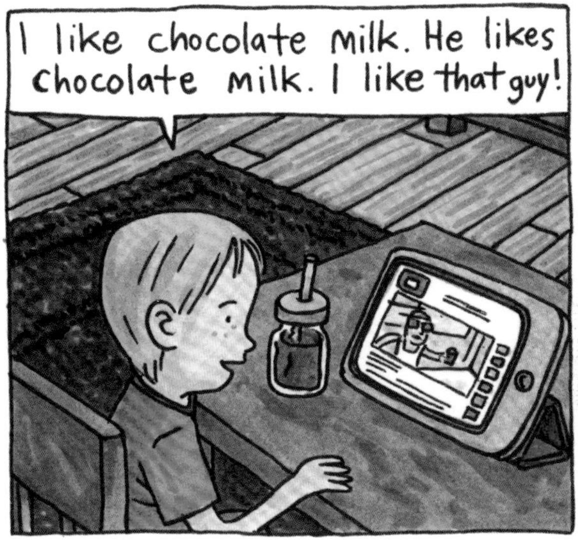
I like chocolate milk. He likes chocolate milk. I like that guy!

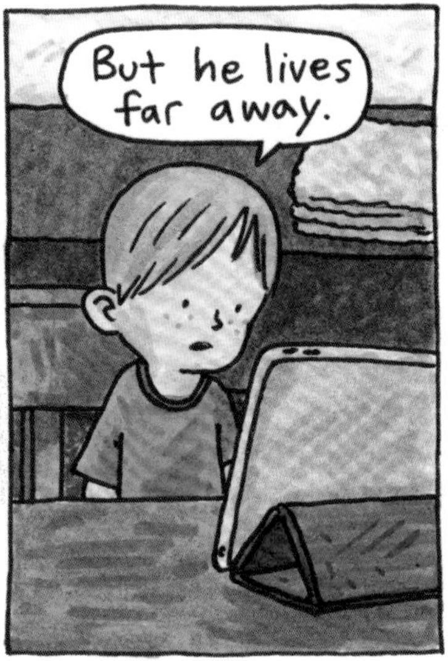
But he lives far away.

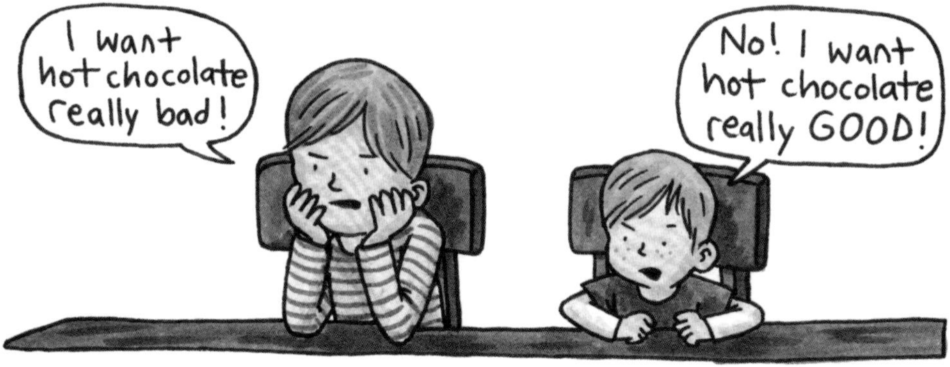
I want hot chocolate really bad!
No! I want hot chocolate really GOOD!

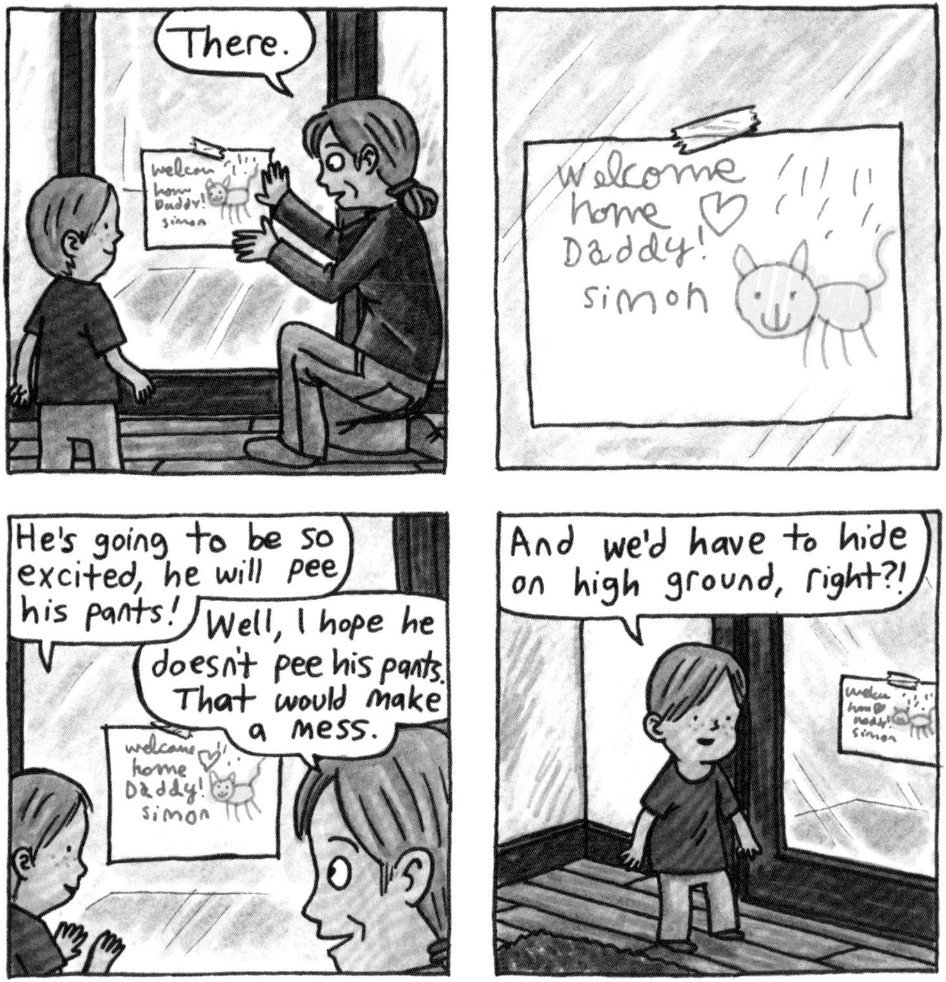
There.
welcome home Daddy! simon
He's going to be so excited, he will pee his pants!
Well, I hope he doesn't pee his pants. That would make a mess.
And we'd have to hide on high ground, right?!

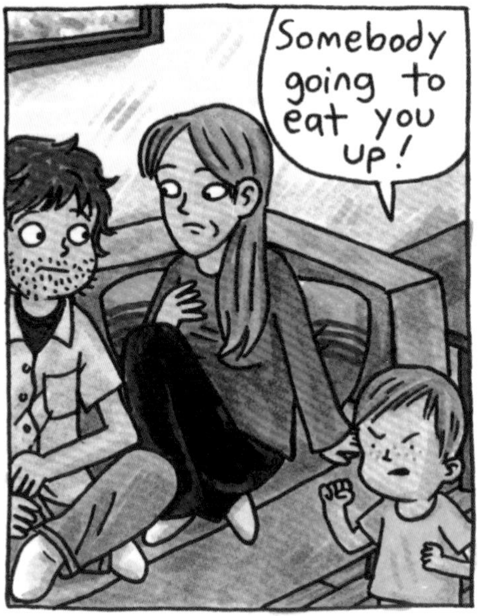
Somebody going to eat you up!

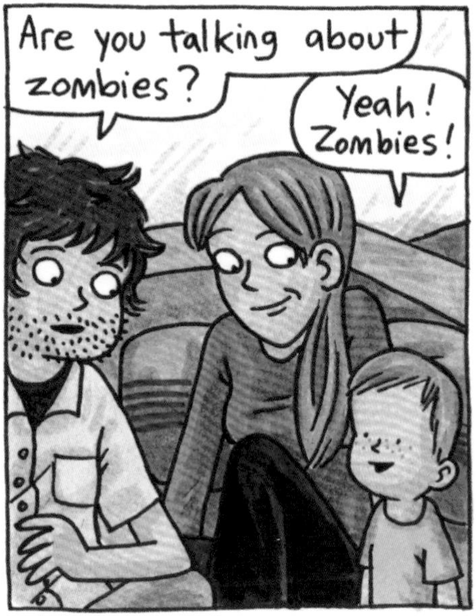
Are you talking about zombies?
Yeah! Zombies!

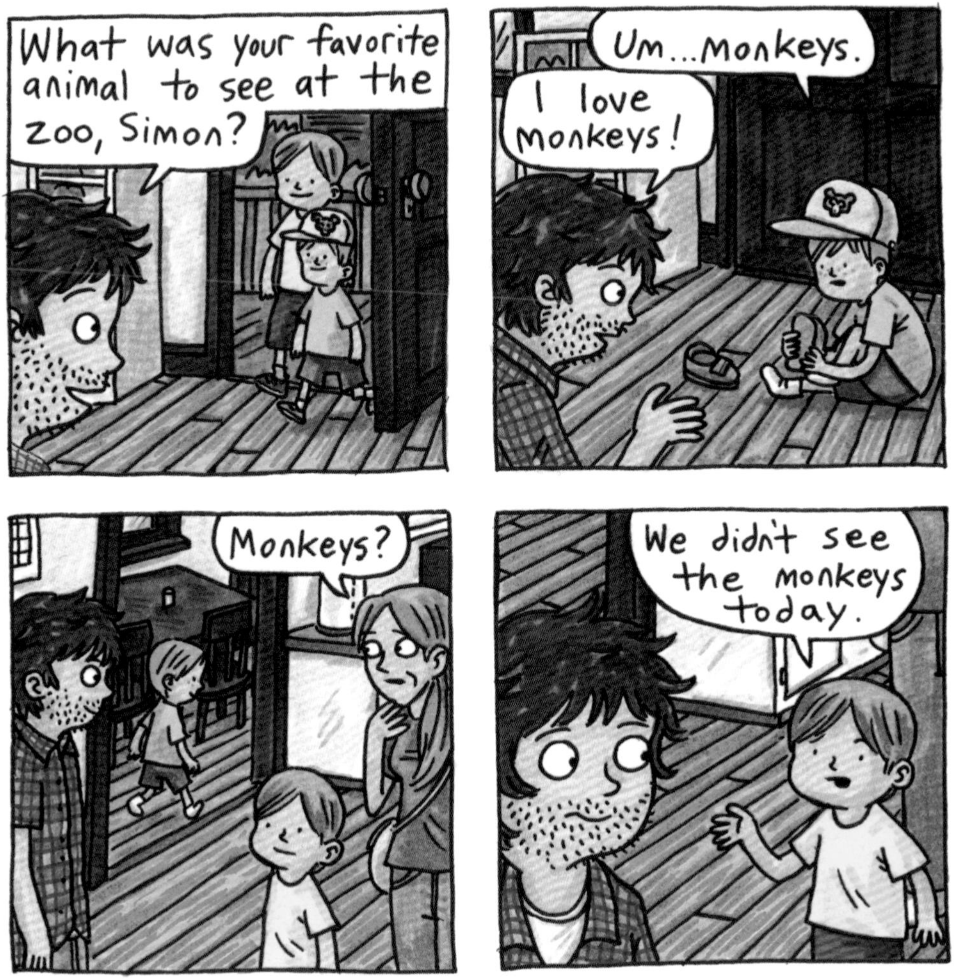
What was your favorite animal to see at the zoo, Simon?
Um...monkeys.
I love monkeys!
Monkeys?
We didn't see the monkeys today.

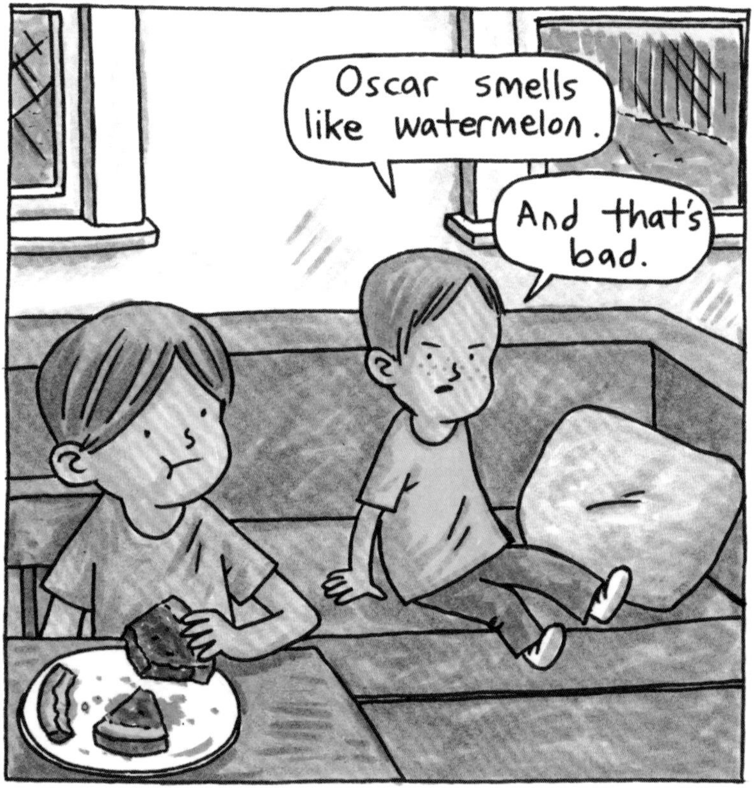
Oscar smells like watermelon.
And that's bad.

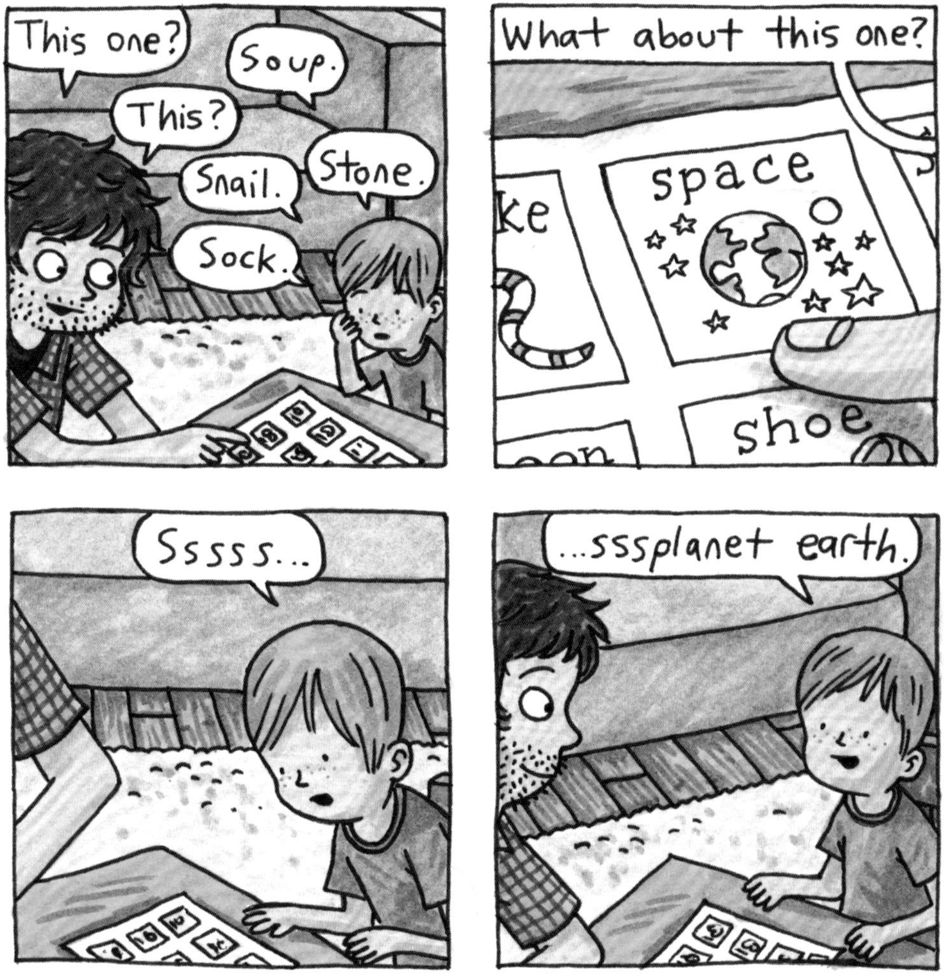
This one?
Soup.
This?
Snail.
Stone.
Sock.
What about this one?
space
shoe
Sssss...
...sssplanet earth.

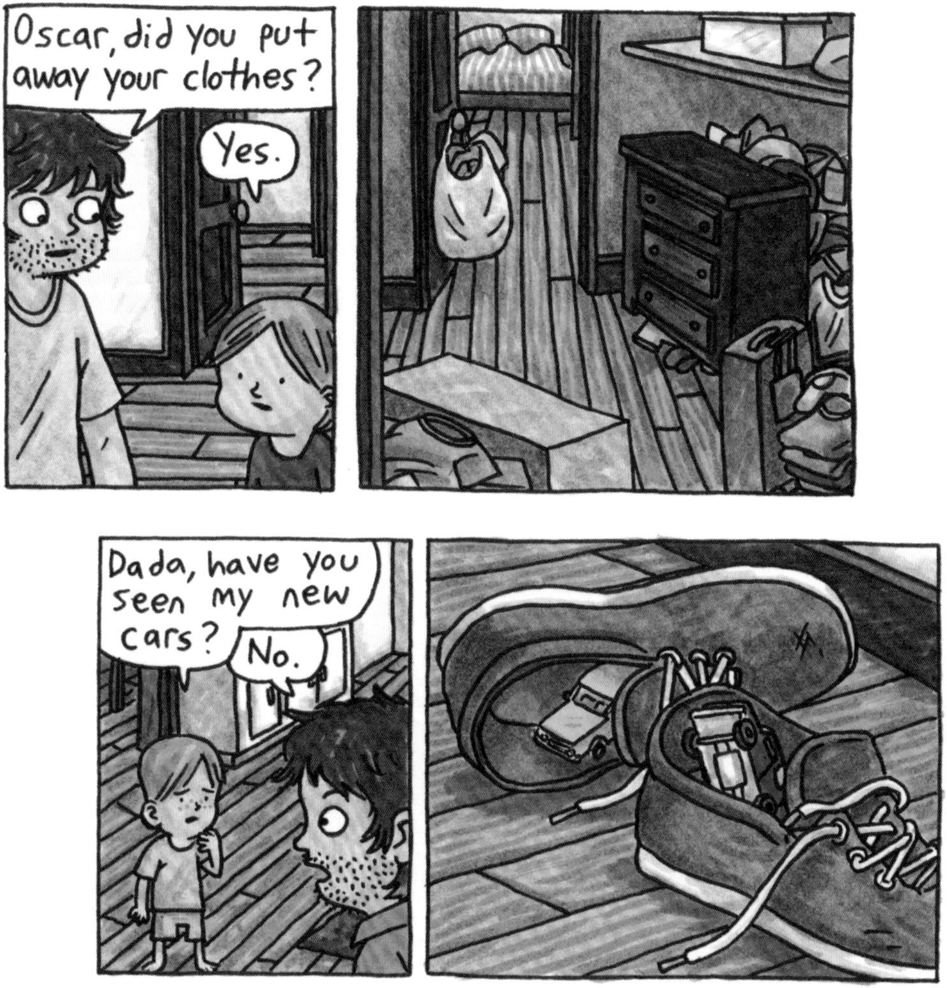
Oscar, did you put away your clothes?
Yes.
Dada, have you seen my new cars?
No.

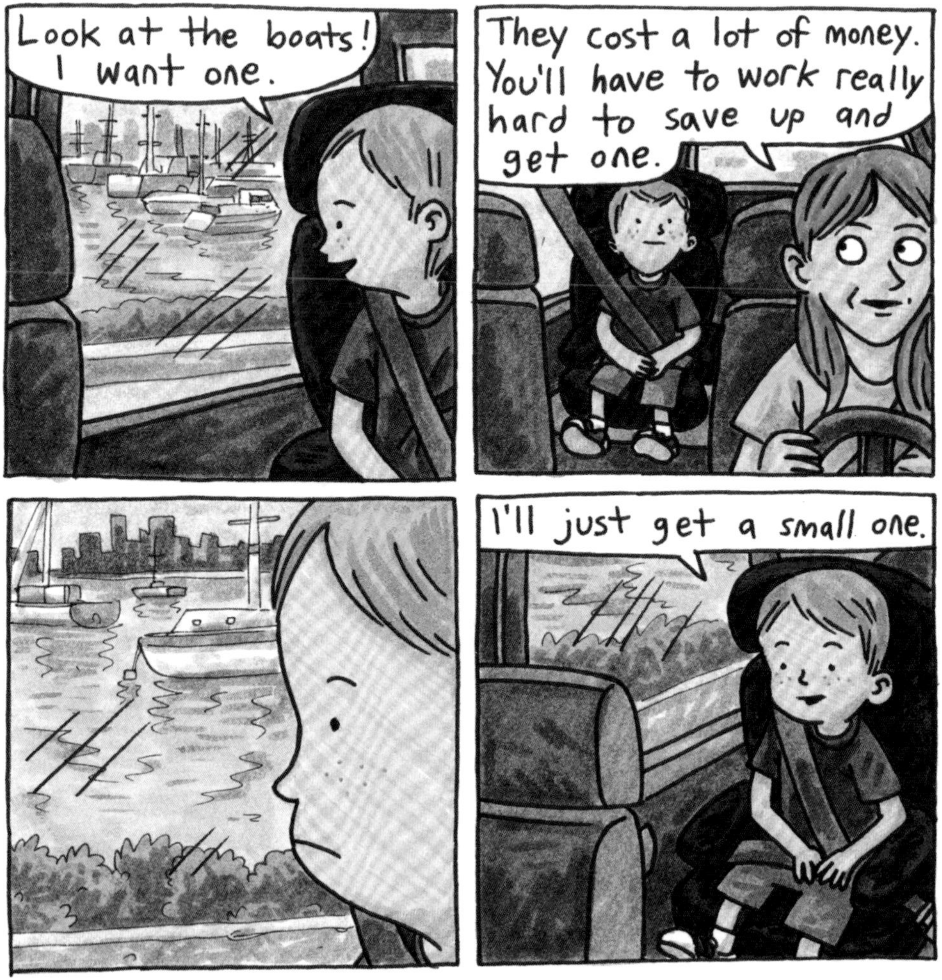
Look at the boats! I want one.
They cost a lot of money. You'll have to work really hard to save up and get one.
I'll just get a small one.

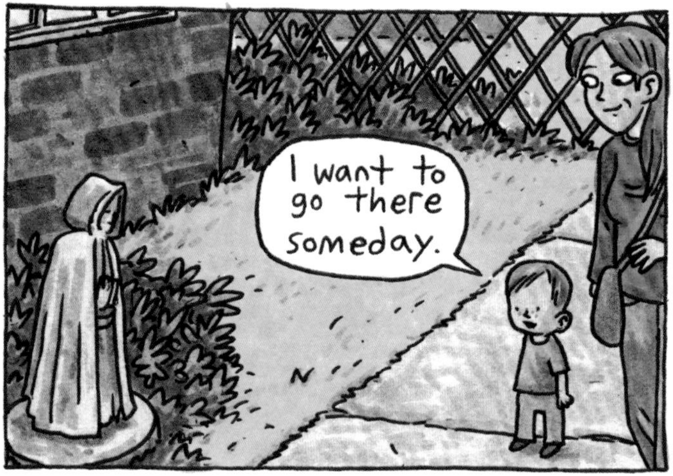
I want to go there someday.

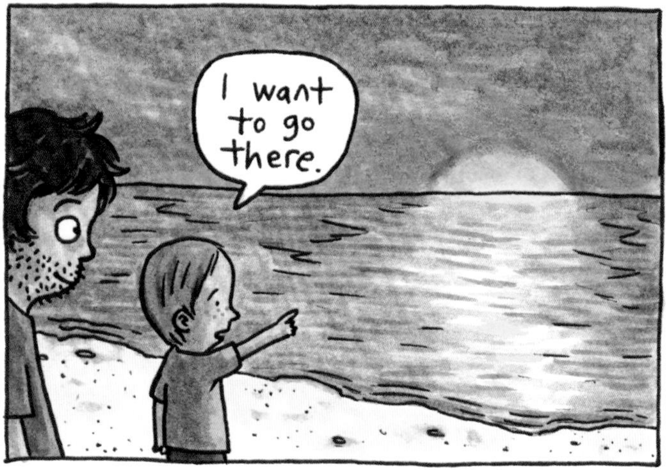
I want to go there.

You put that idea into my head.

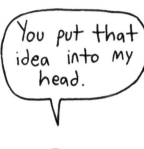

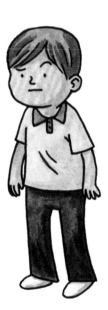

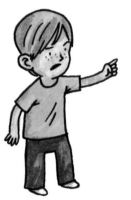

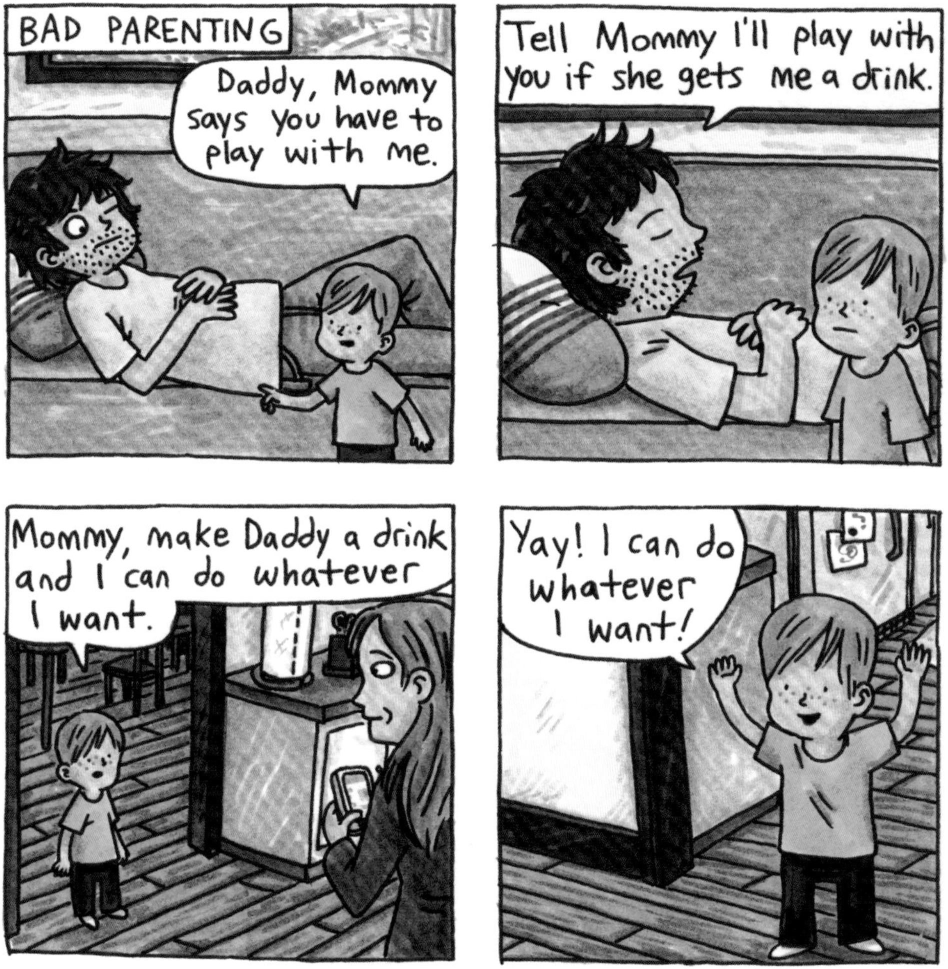
BAD PARENTING
Daddy, Mommy says you have to play with me.
Tell Mommy I'll play with you if she gets me a drink.
Mommy, make Daddy a drink and I can do whatever I want.
Yay! I can do whatever I want!

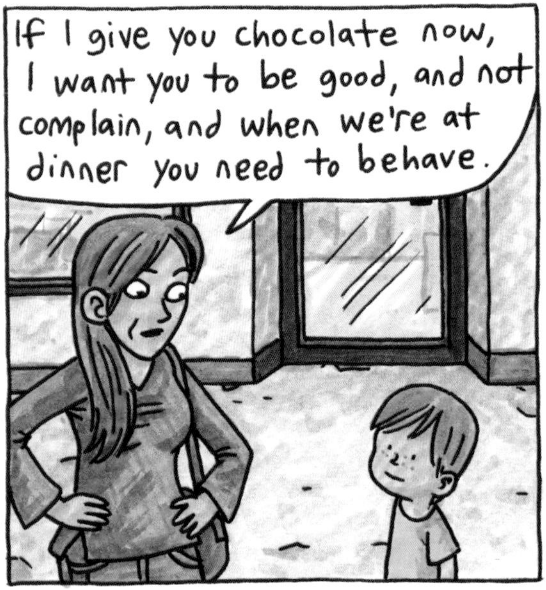
If I give you chocolate now, I want you to be good, and not complain, and when we're at dinner you need to behave.

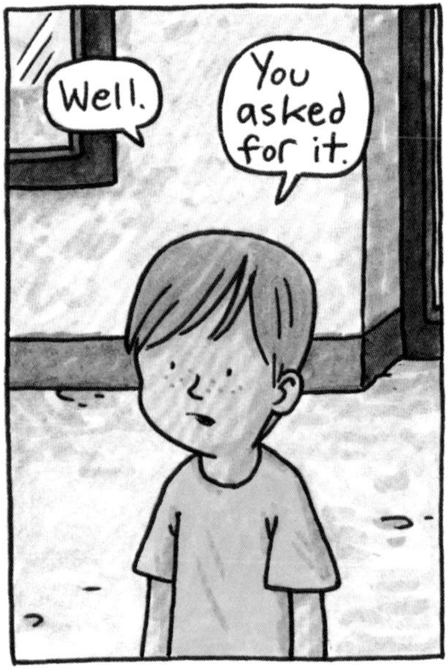
Well.
You asked for it.

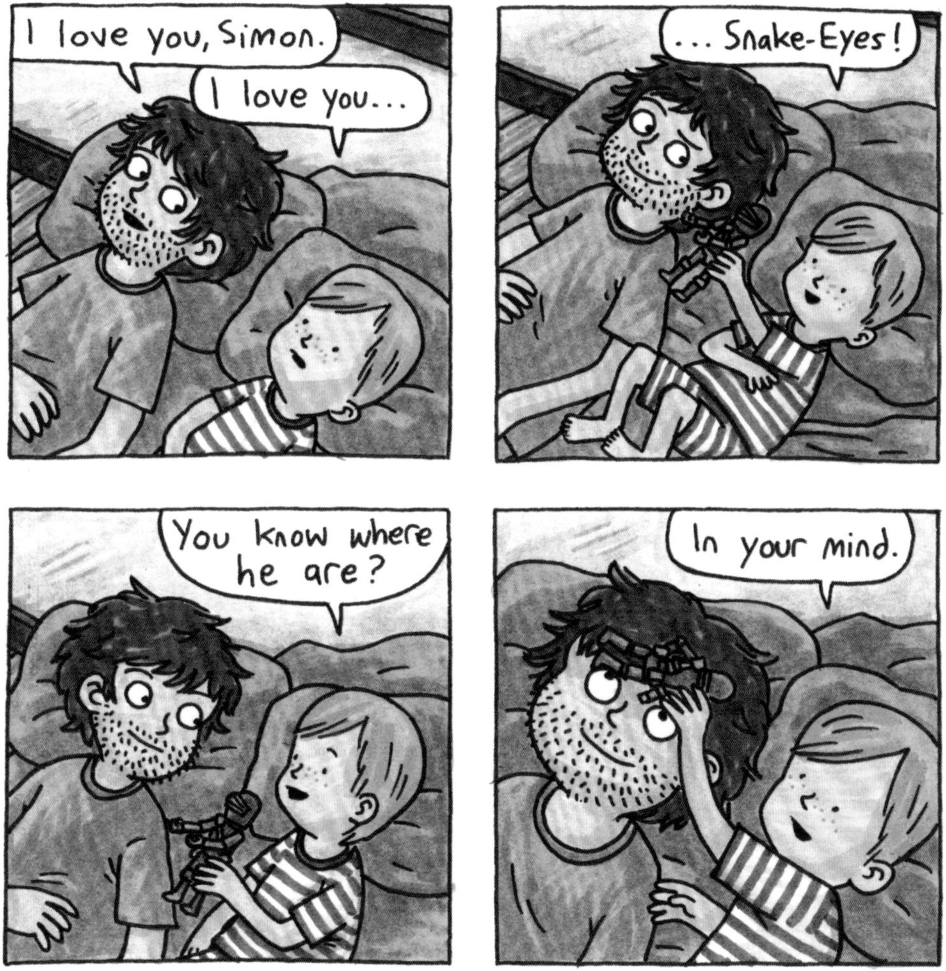
I love you, Simon.
I love you...
... Snake-Eyes!
You know where he are?
In your mind.

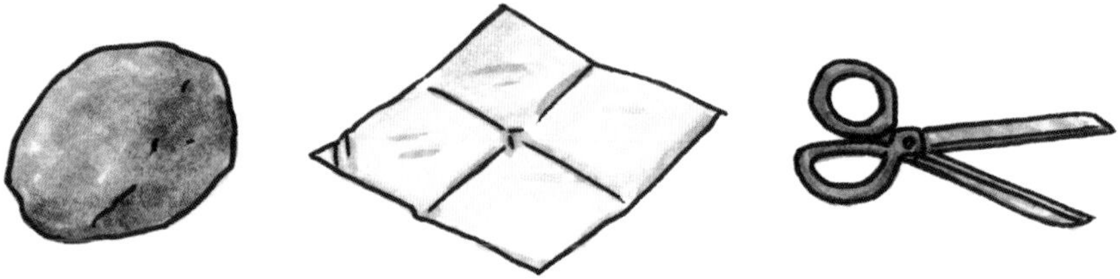

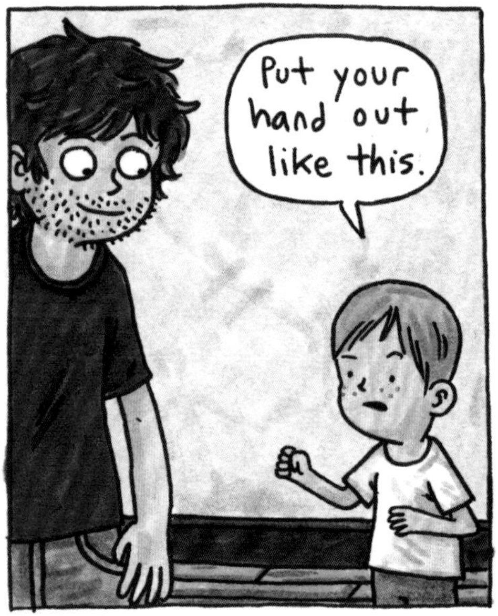
Put your hand out like this.

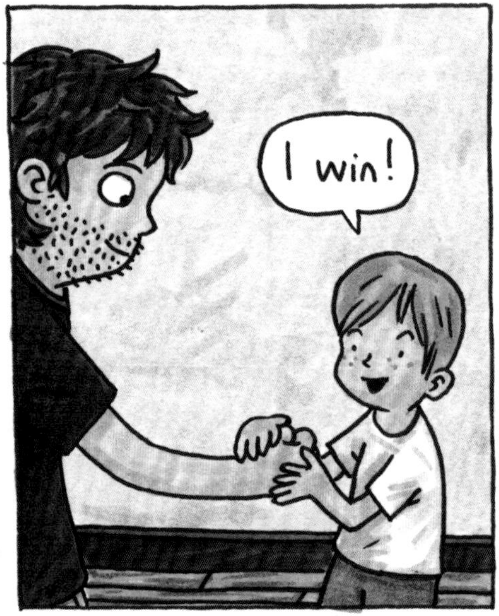
I win!

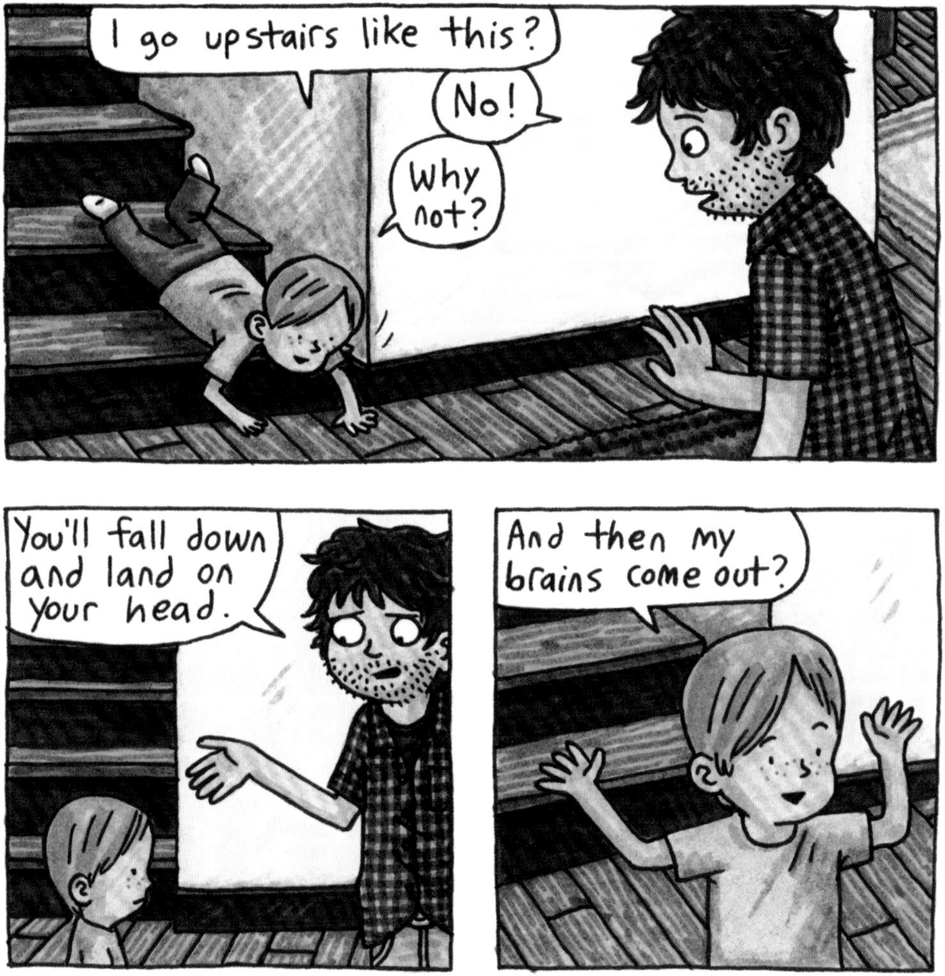
I go upstairs like this?
No!
Why not?
You'll fall down and land on your head.
And then my brains come out?

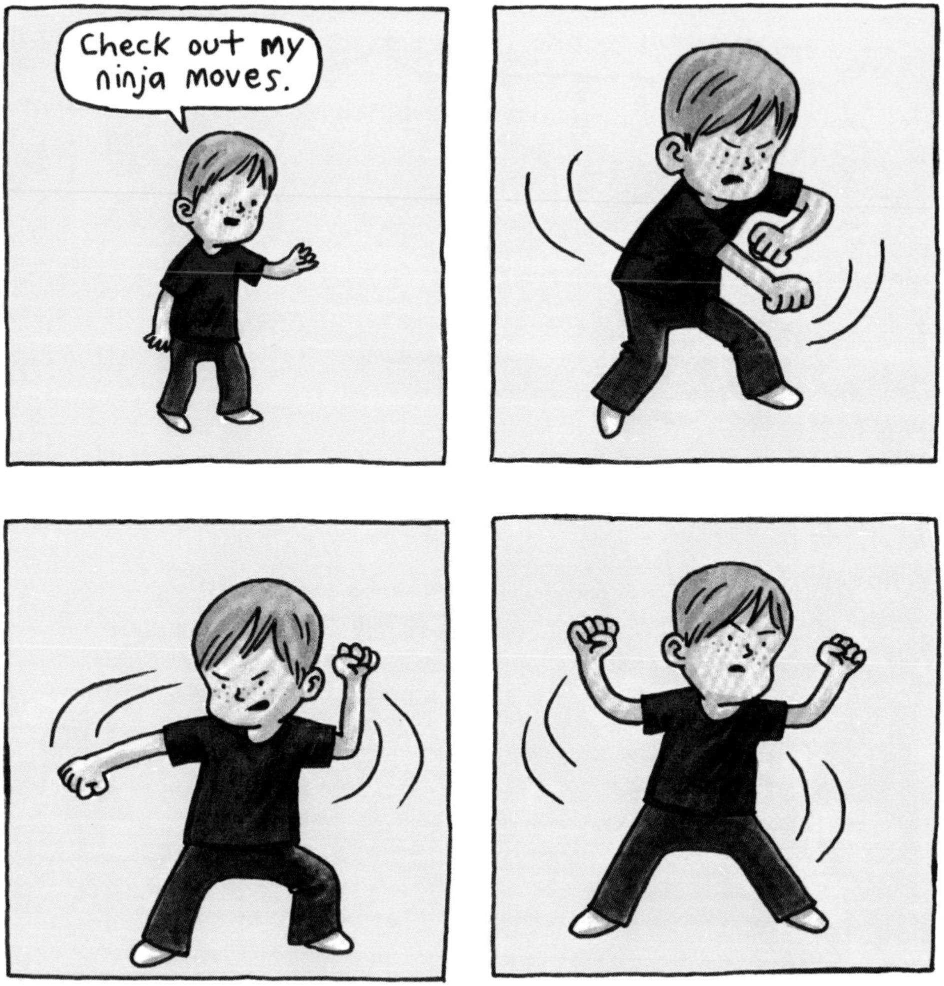
Check out my ninja moves.

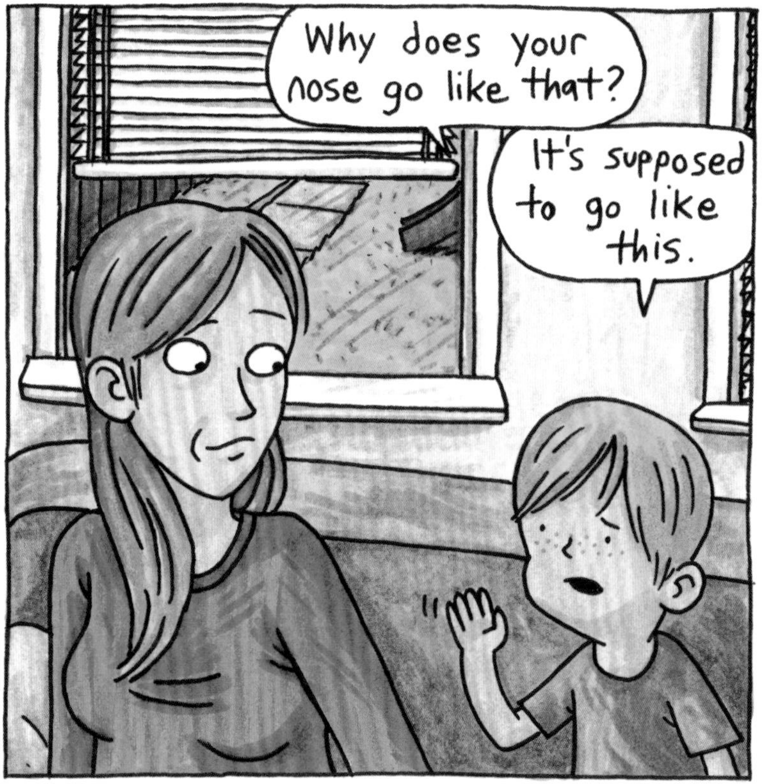
Why does your nose go like that?
It's supposed to go like this.

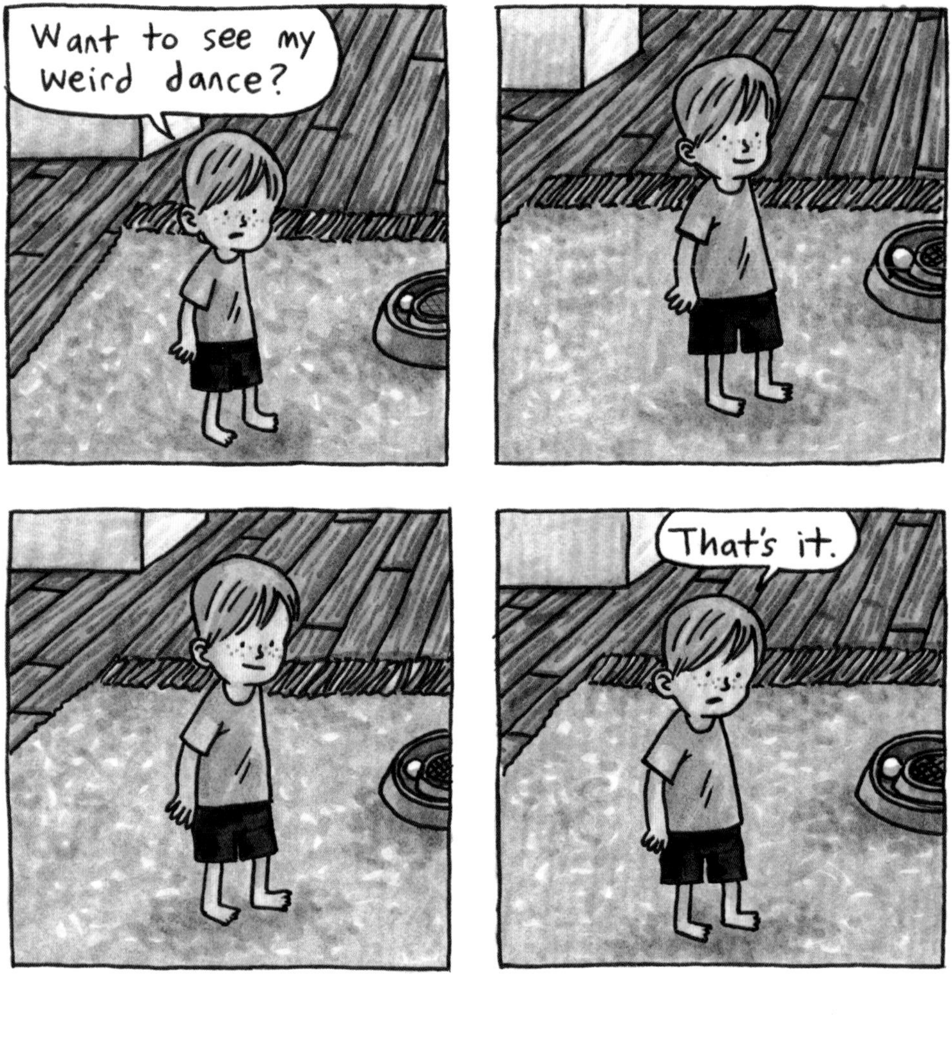
Want to see my weird dance?
That's it.

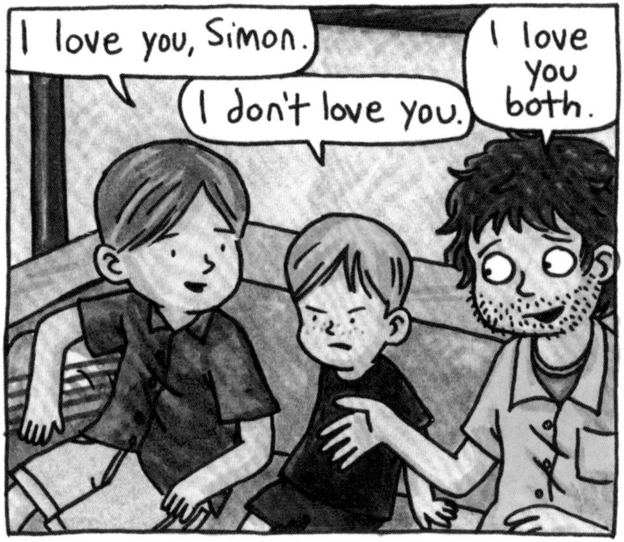
I love you, Simon.
I don't love you.
I love you both.

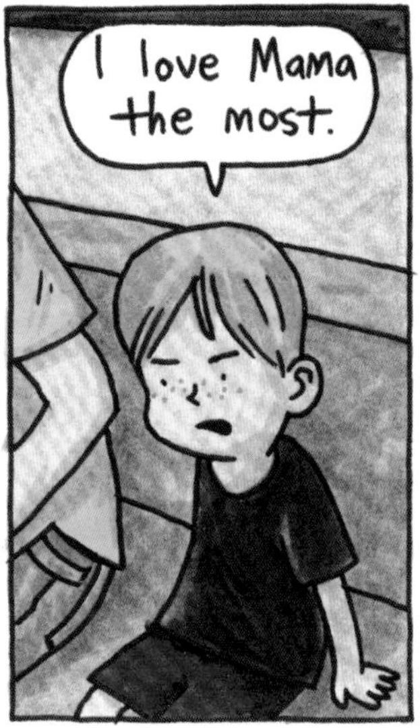
I love Mama the most.

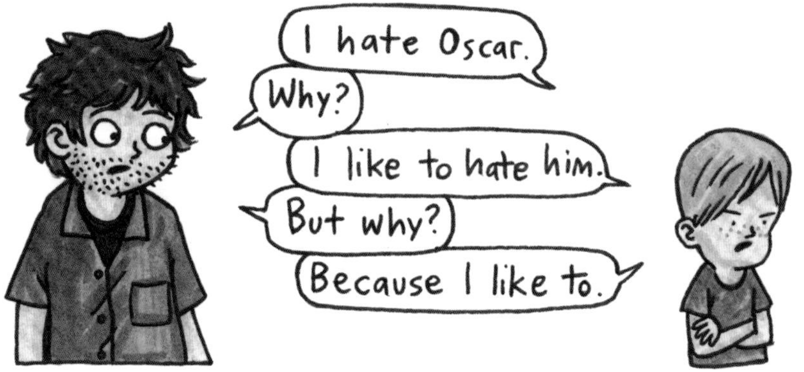
I hate Oscar.
Why?
I like to hate him.
But why?
Because I like to.

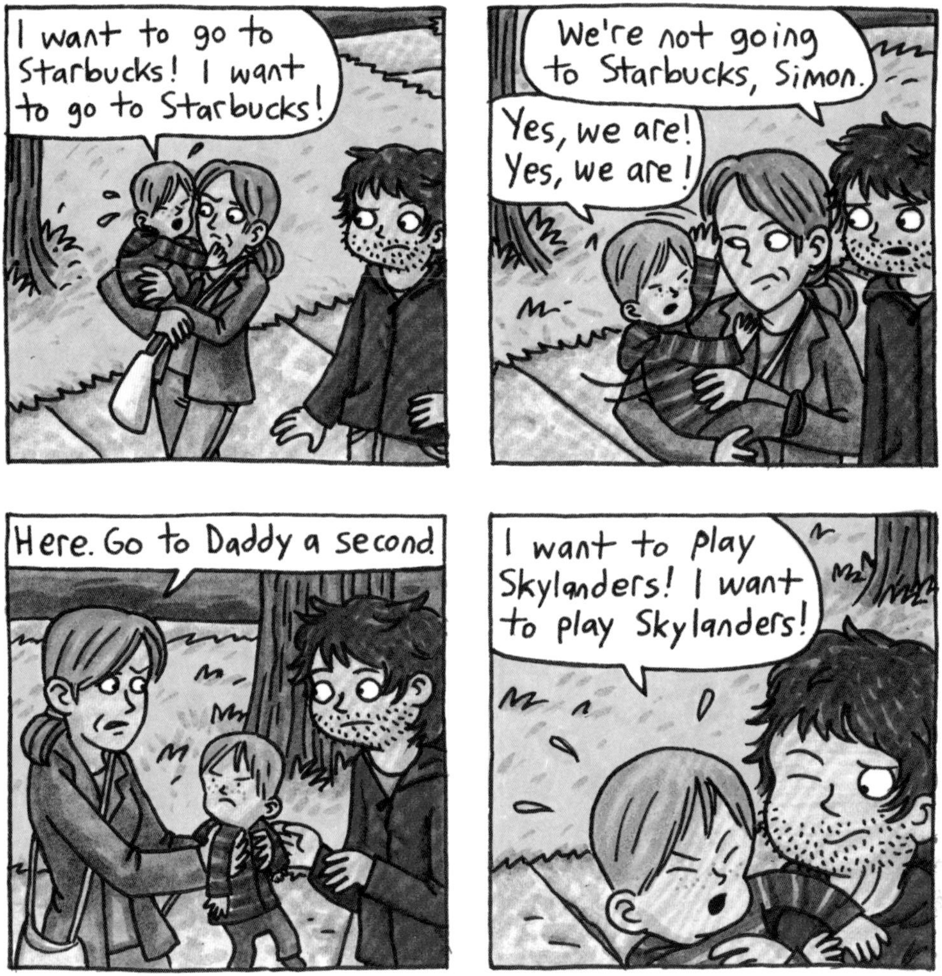
I want to go to Starbucks! I want to go to Starbucks!
We're not going to Starbucks, Simon.
Yes, we are! Yes, we are!
Here. Go to Daddy a second.
I want to play Skylanders! I want to play Skylanders!

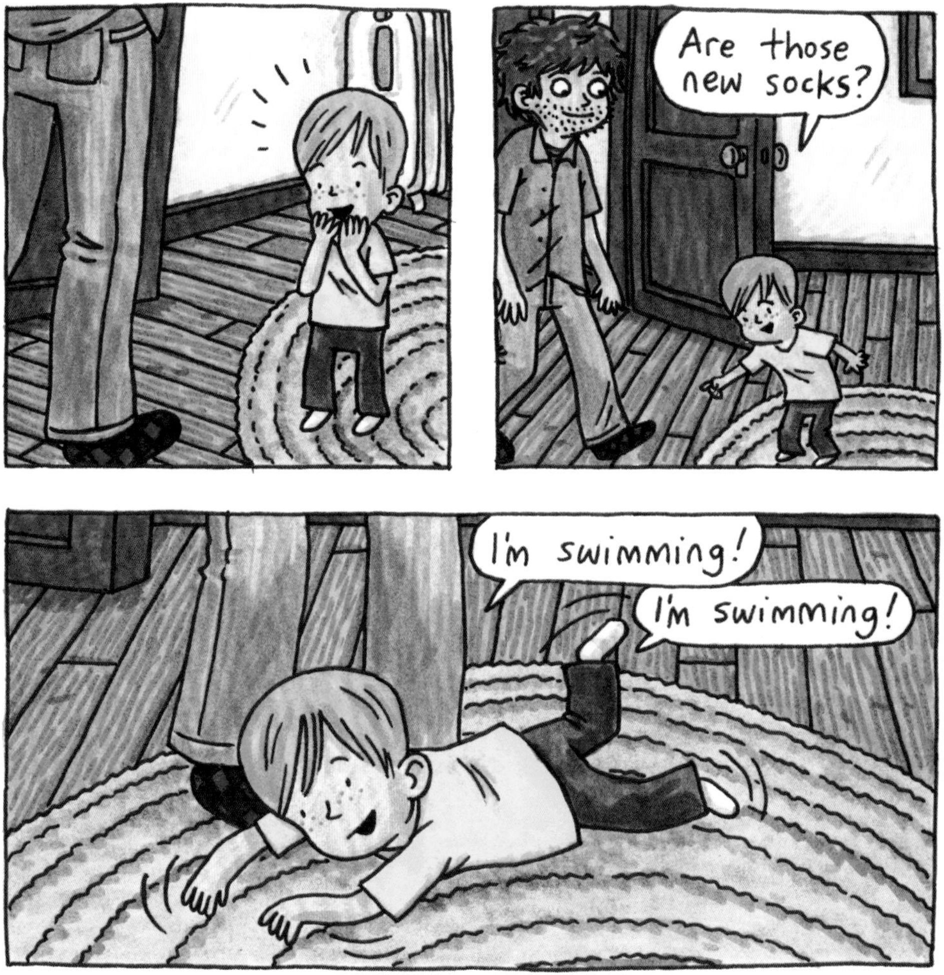
Are those new socks?
I'm swimming!
I'm swimming!

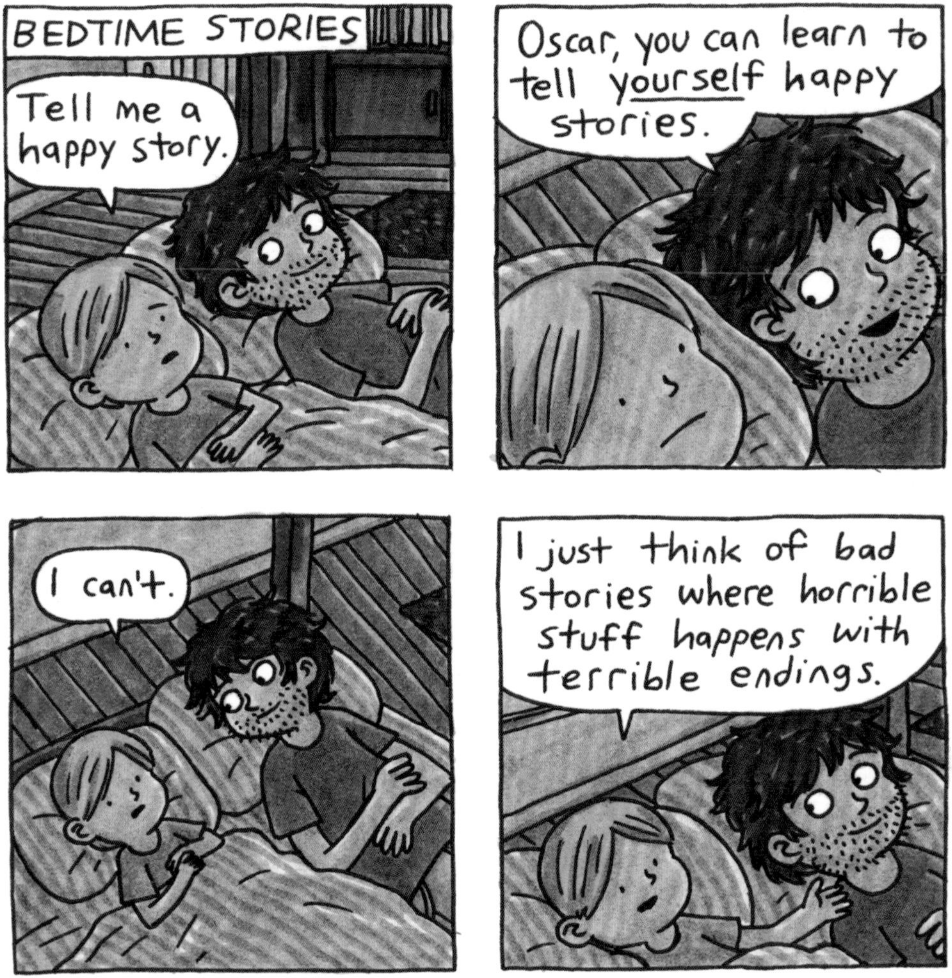
BEDTIME STORIES
Tell me a happy story.
Oscar, you can learn to tell yourself happy stories.
I can't.
I just think of bad stories where horrible stuff happens with terrible endings.

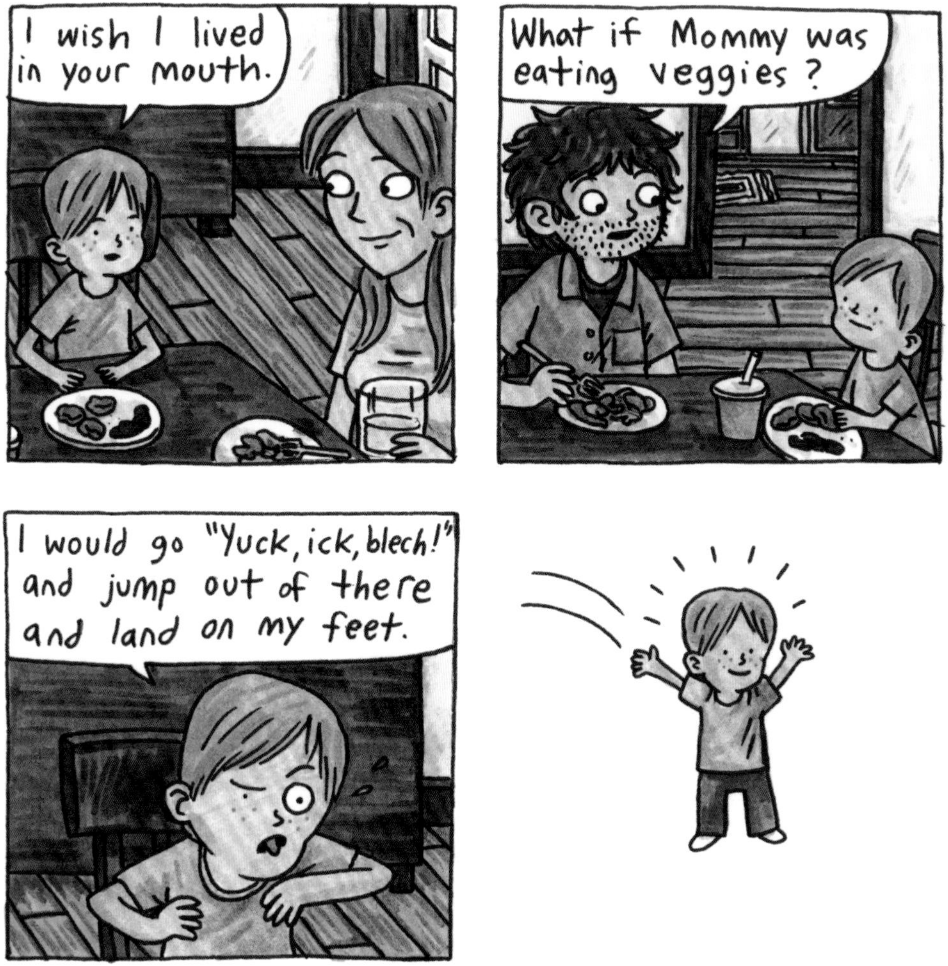
I wish I lived in your mouth.
What if Mommy was eating veggies?
I would go "Yuck, ick, blech!" and jump out of there and land on my feet.

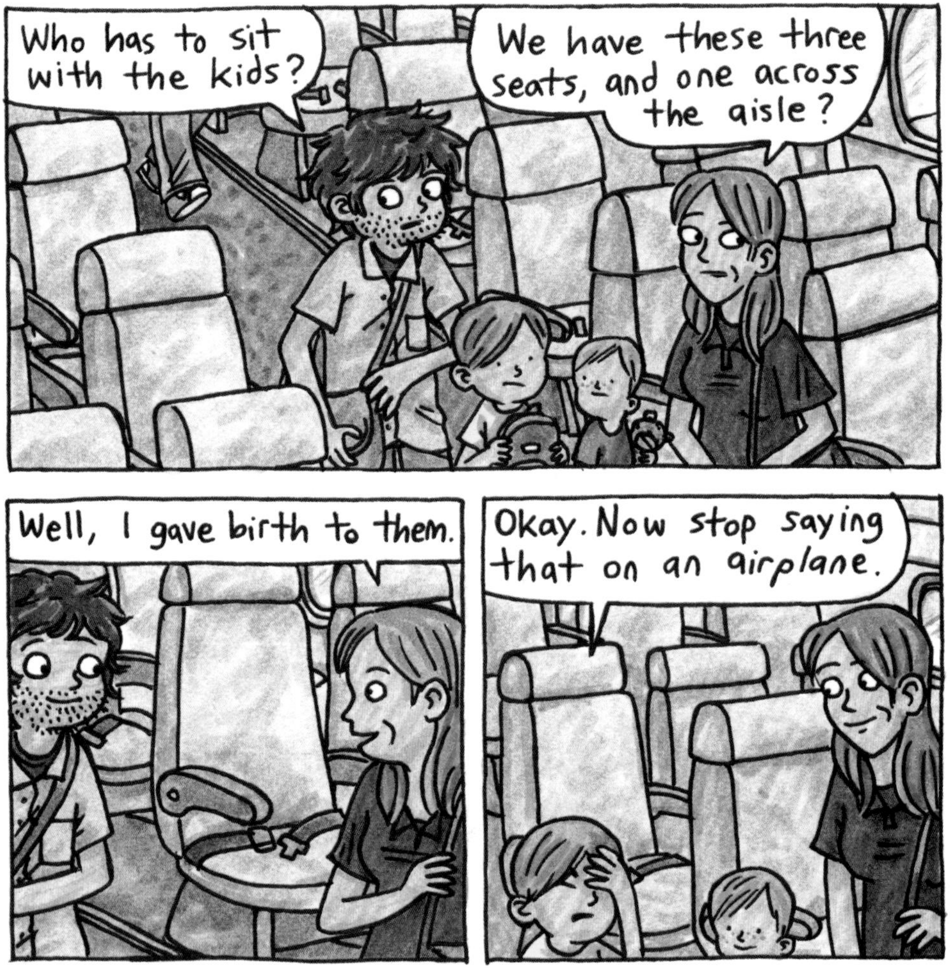
Who has to sit with the kids?
We have these three seats, and one across the aisle?
Well, I gave birth to them.
Okay. Now stop saying that on an airplane.

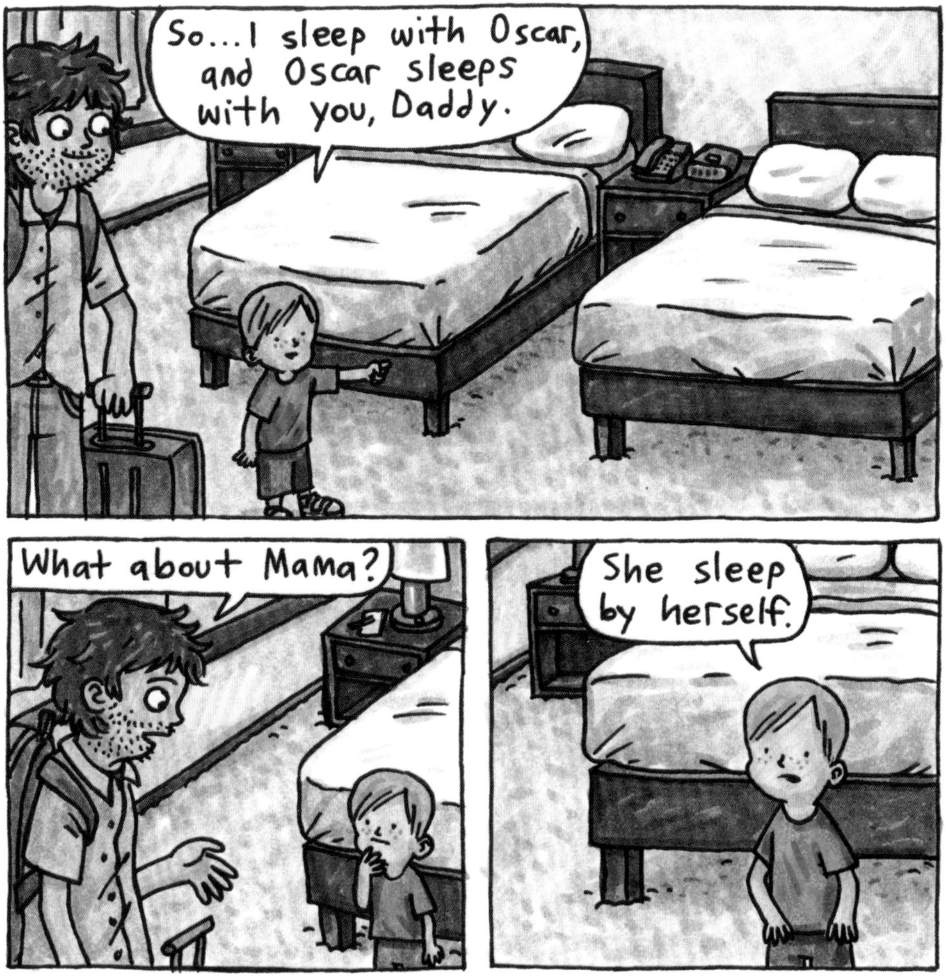
So...I sleep with Oscar, and Oscar sleeps with you, Daddy.
What about Mama?
She sleep by herself.

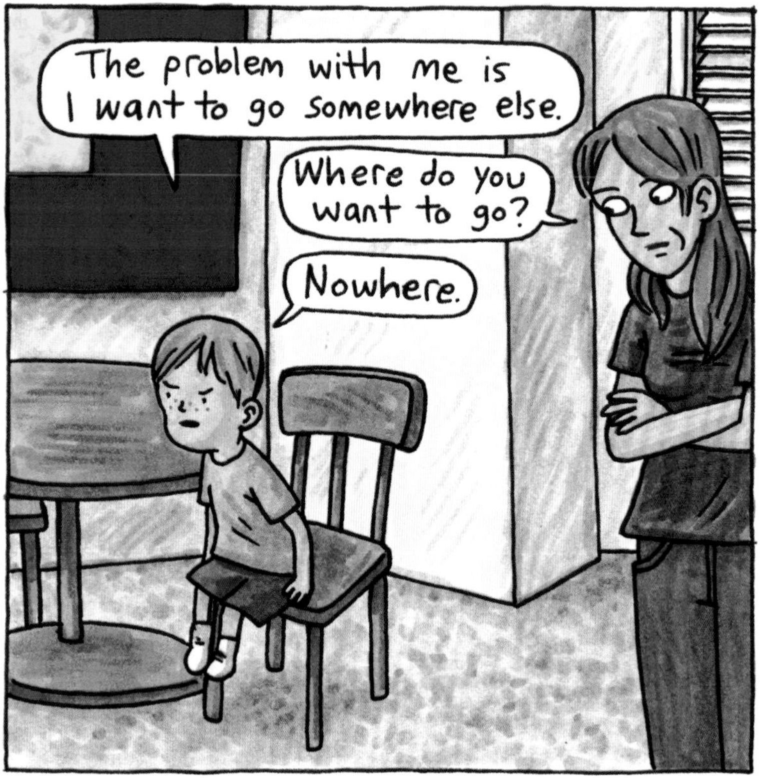
The problem with me is I want to go somewhere else.
Where do you want to go?
Nowhere.

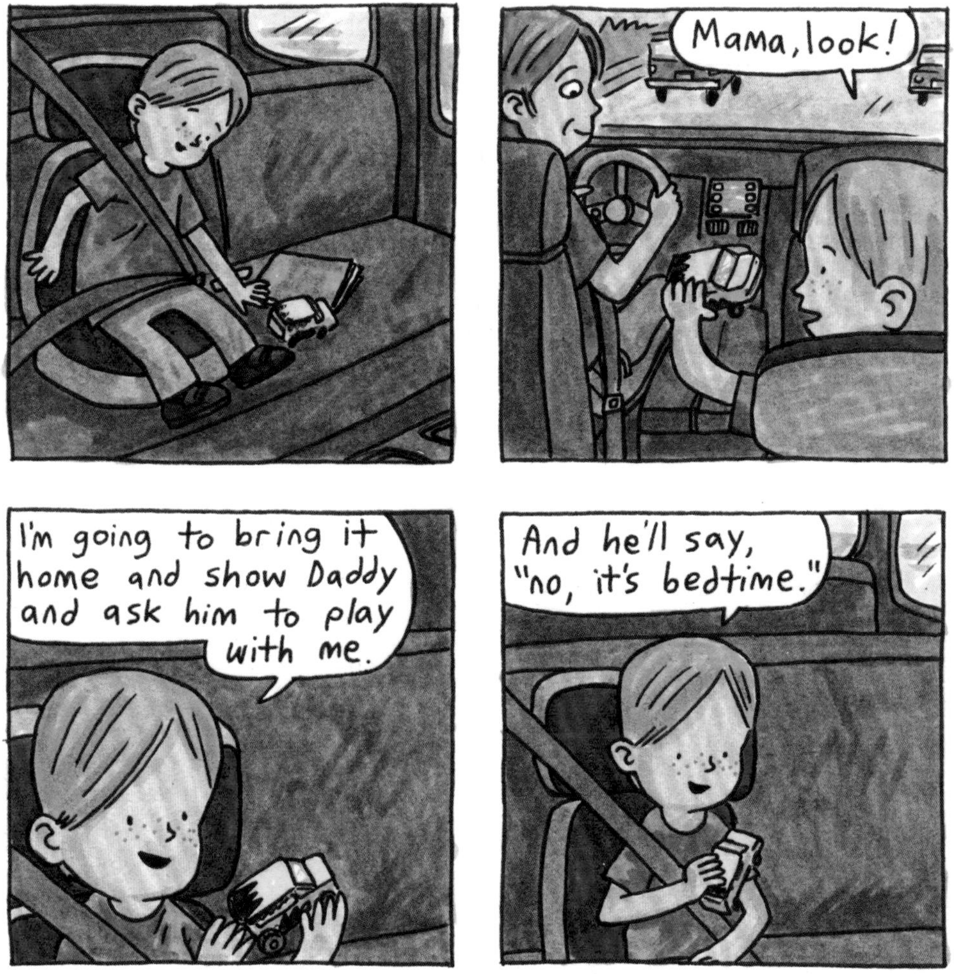
Mama, look!
I'm going to bring it home and show Daddy and ask him to play with me.
And he'll say, "no, it's bedtime."

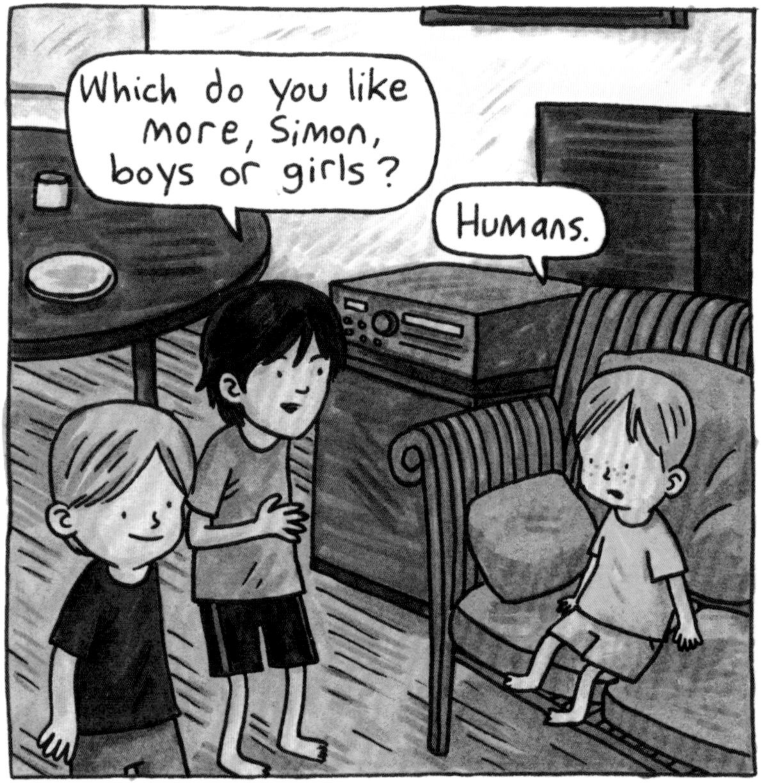
Which do you like more, Simon, boys or girls?
Humans.

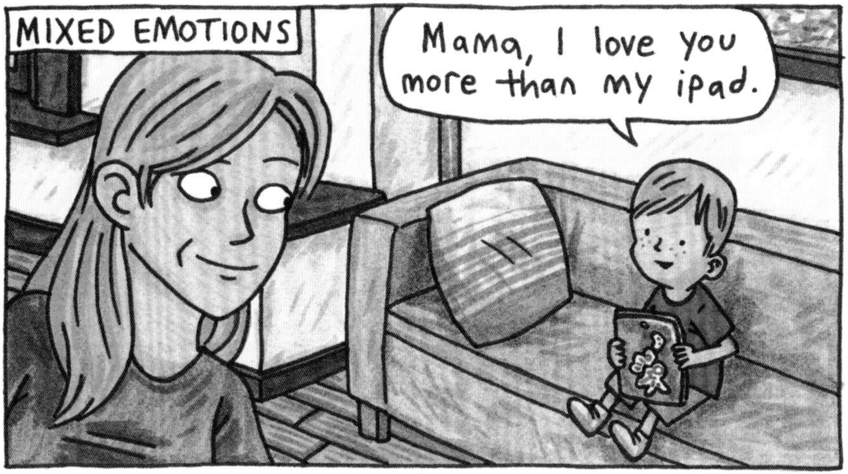
MIXED EMOTIONS
Mama, I love you more than my ipad.

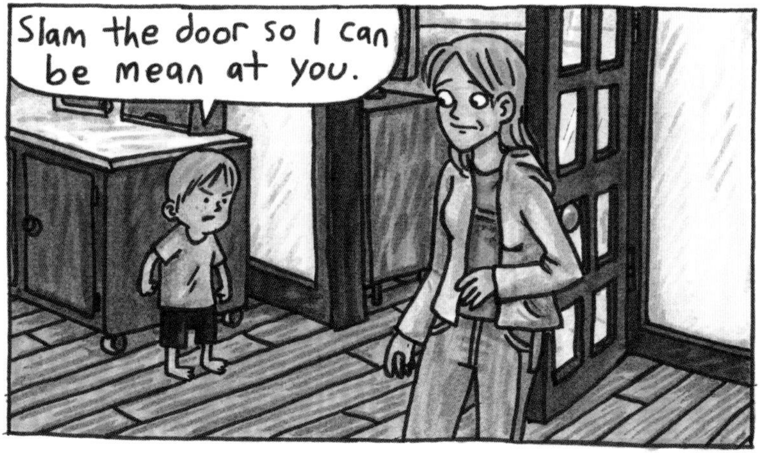
Slam the door so I can be mean at you.

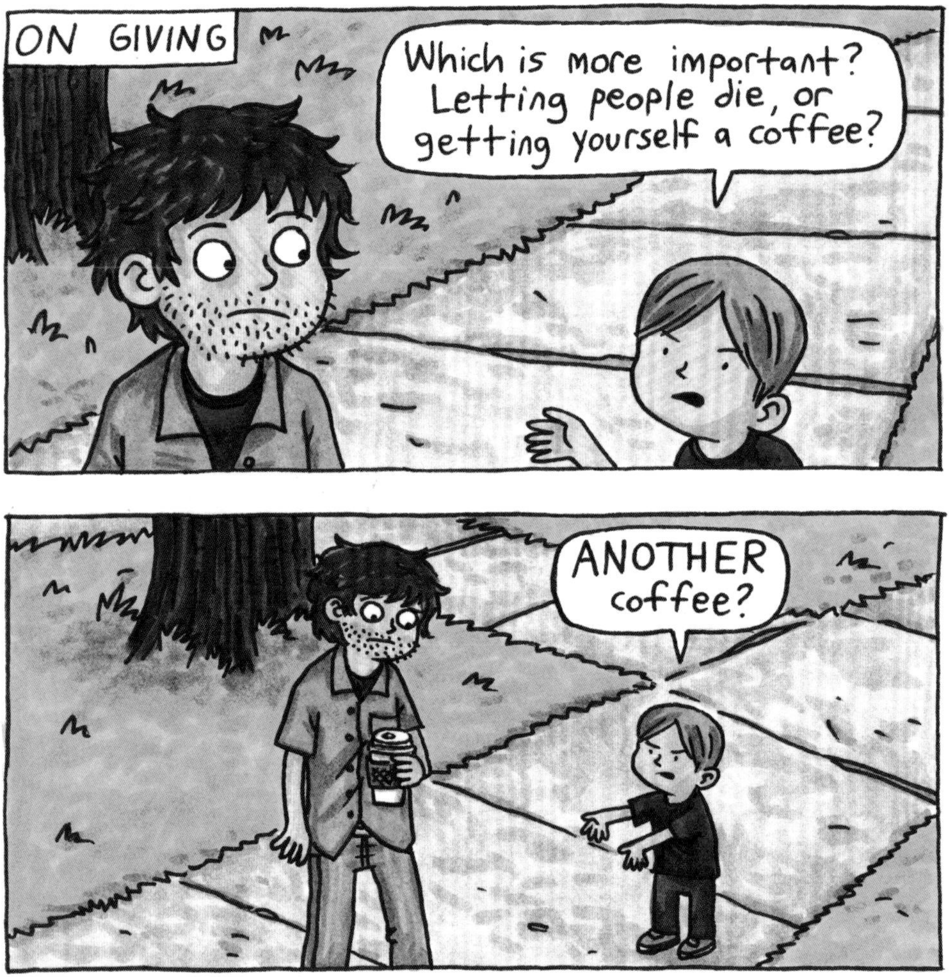
ON GIVING
Which is more important? Letting people die, or getting yourself a coffee?
ANOTHER coffee?

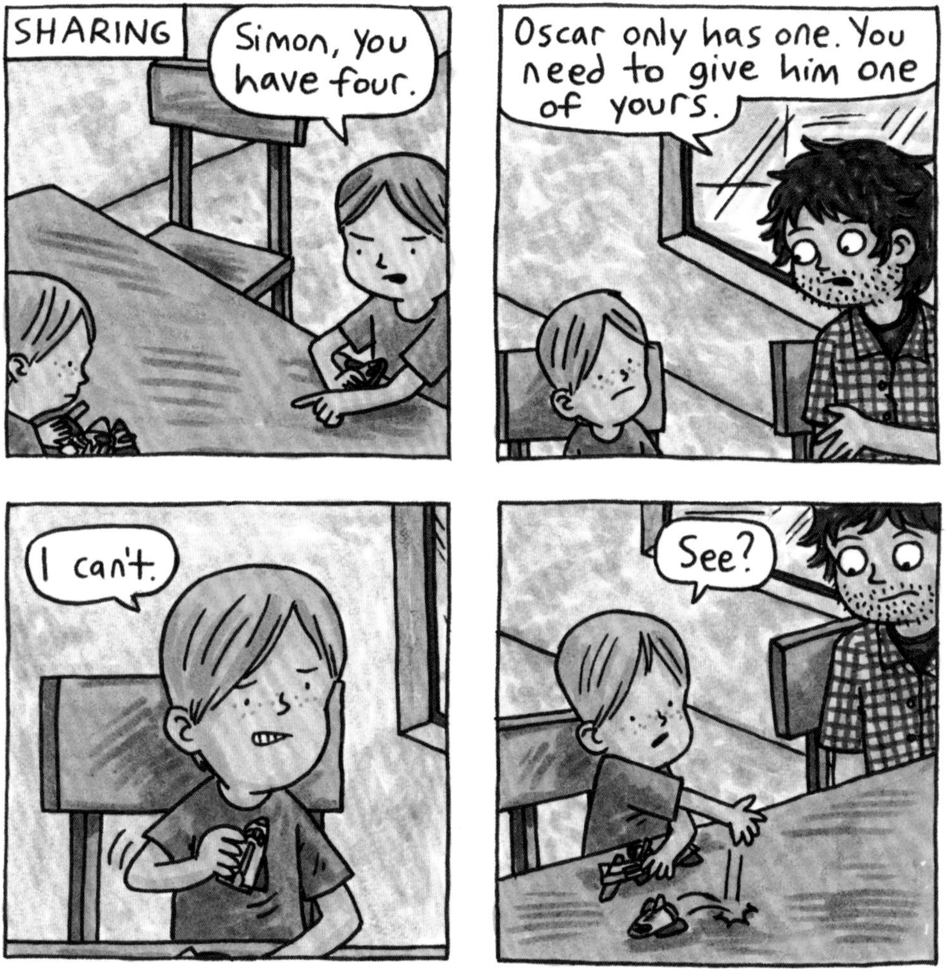
SHARING
Simon, you have four.
Oscar only has one. You need to give him one of yours.
I can't.
See?

I'm in charge! Look at my shirt. It says I'm in charge. Not Dada, not Mama, not Oscar. I'm in charge. Not you. Me. Not anybody.

Look at my shirt.

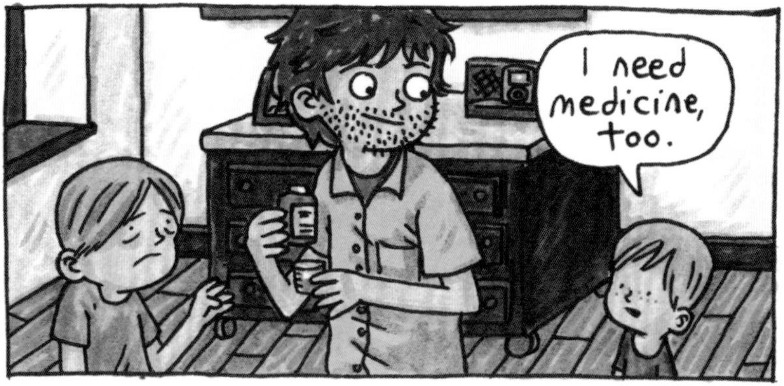
I need medicine, too.

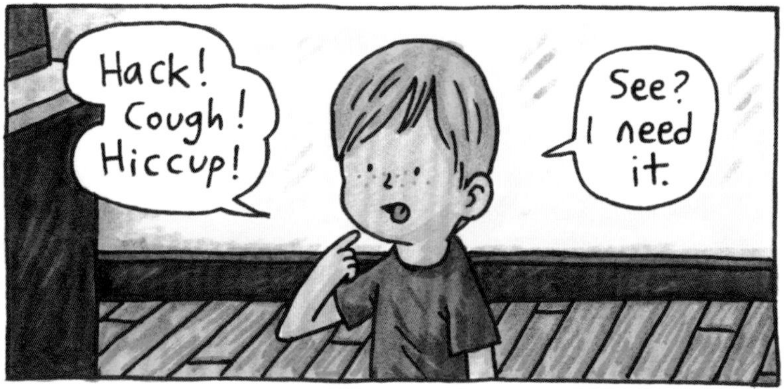
Hack! Cough! Hiccup!
See? I need it.

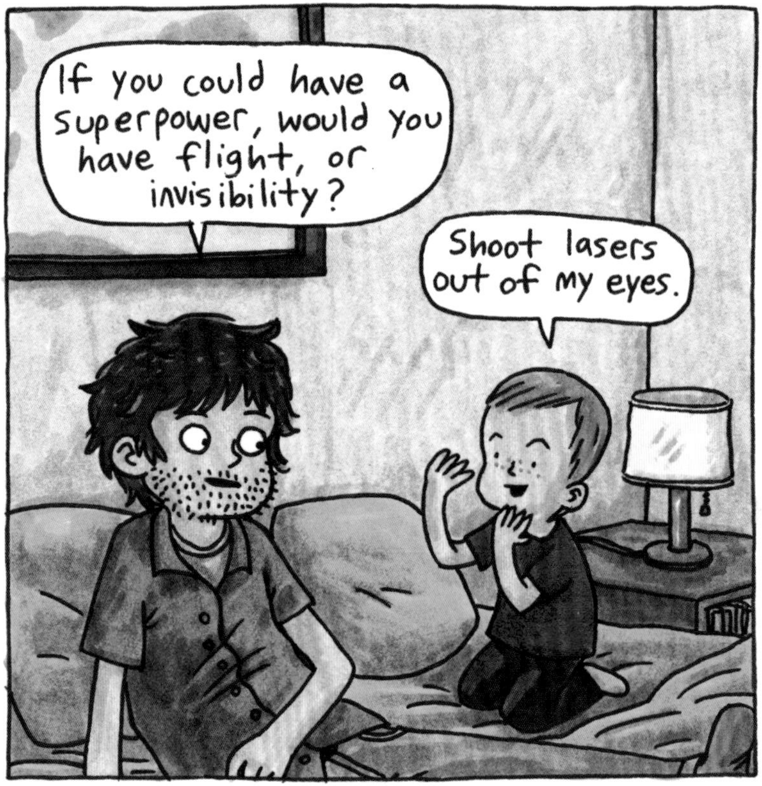
If you could have a superpower, would you have flight, or invisibility?
Shoot lasers out of my eyes.

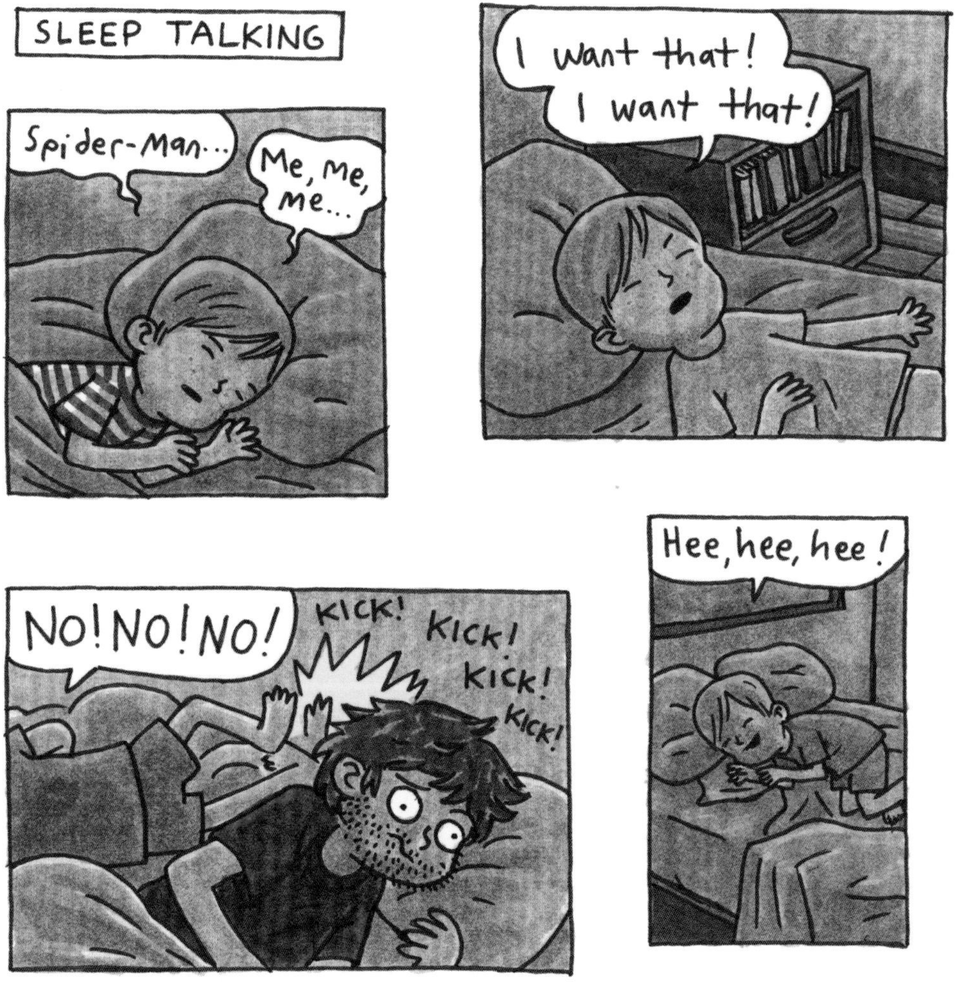
SLEEP TALKING
Spider-Man...
Me, me, me...
I want that! I want that!
NO! NO! NO!
KICK! KICK! KICK! KICK!
Hee, hee, hee!

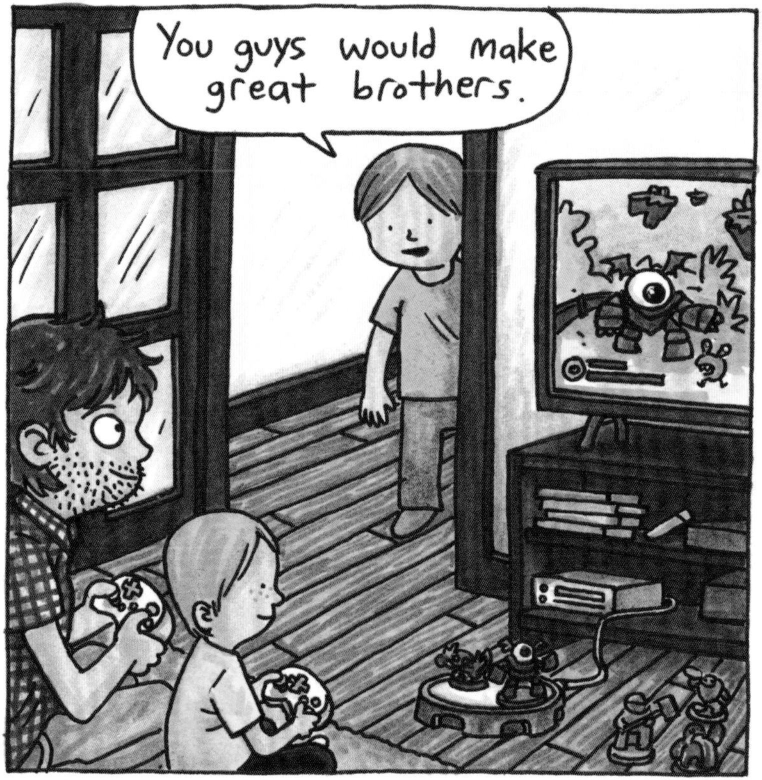
You guys would make great brothers.

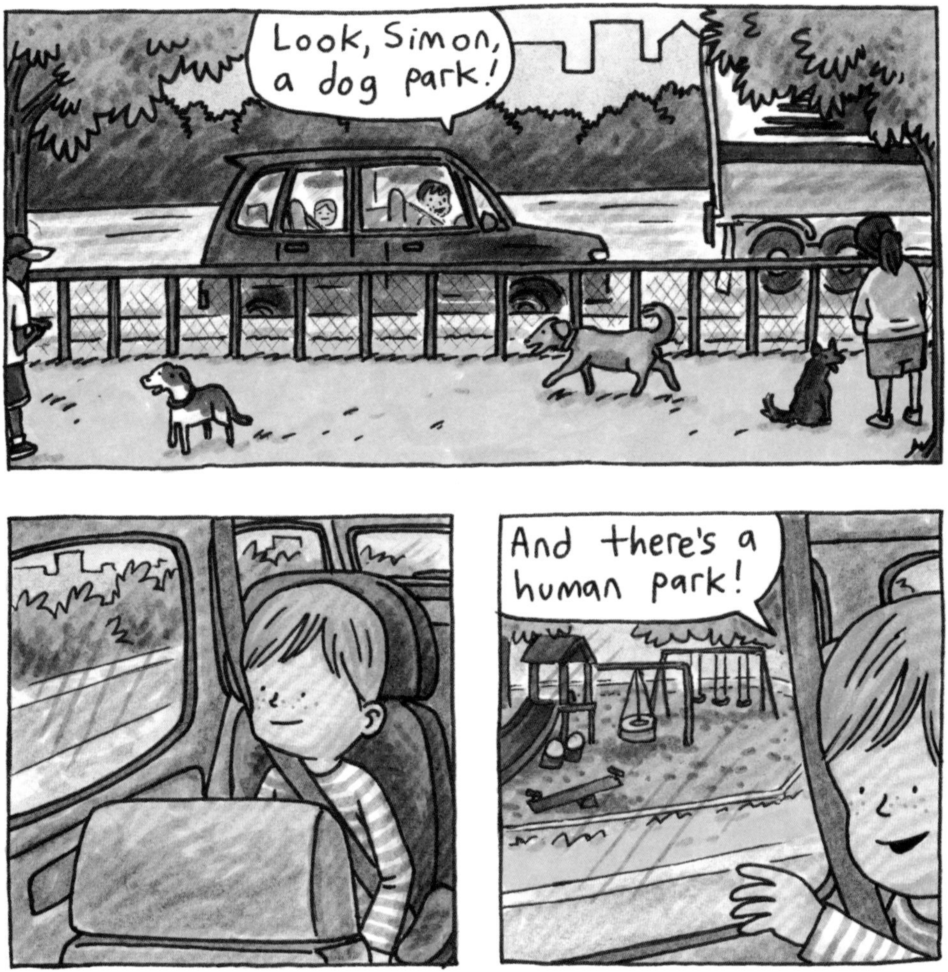
Look, Simon, a dog park!
And there's a human park!

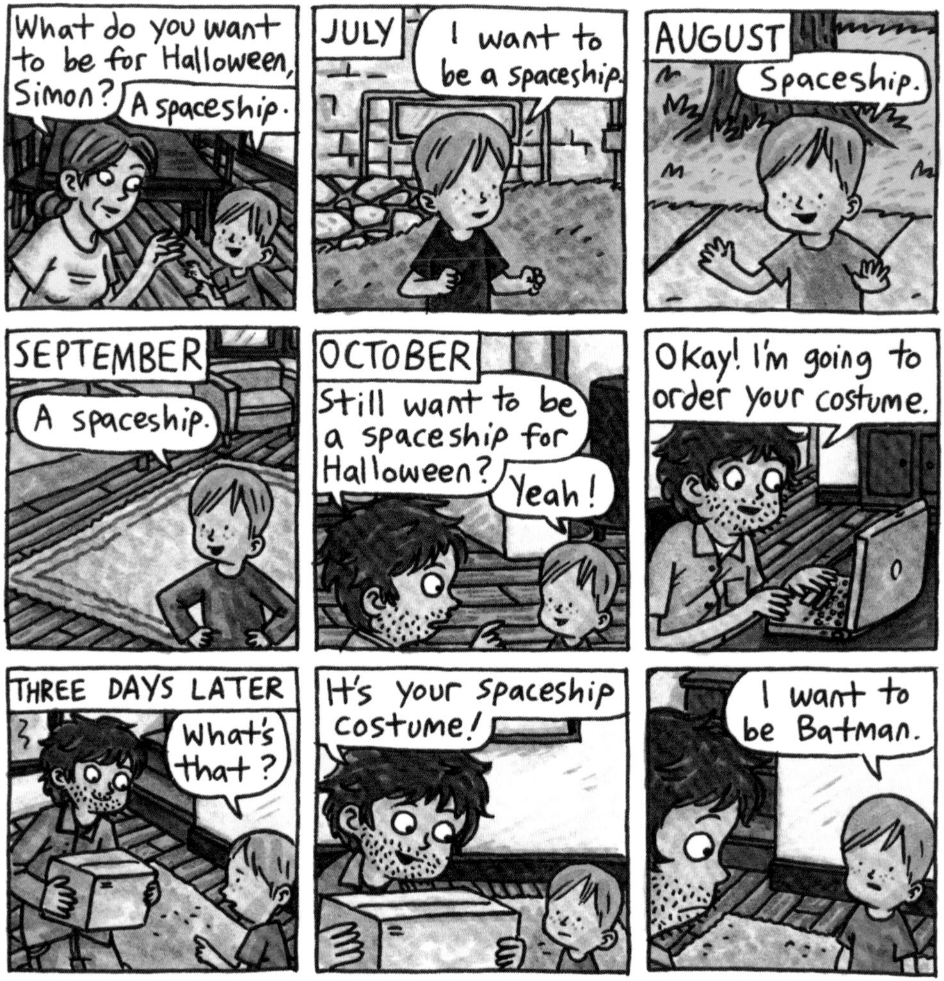
What do you want to be for Halloween, Simon?
A spaceship.
JULY
I want to be a spaceship.
AUGUST
Spaceship.
SEPTEMBER
A spaceship.
OCTOBER
Still want to be a spaceship for Halloween?
Yeah!
Okay! I'm going to order your costume.
THREE DAYS LATER
What's that?
It's your spaceship costume!
I want to be Batman.

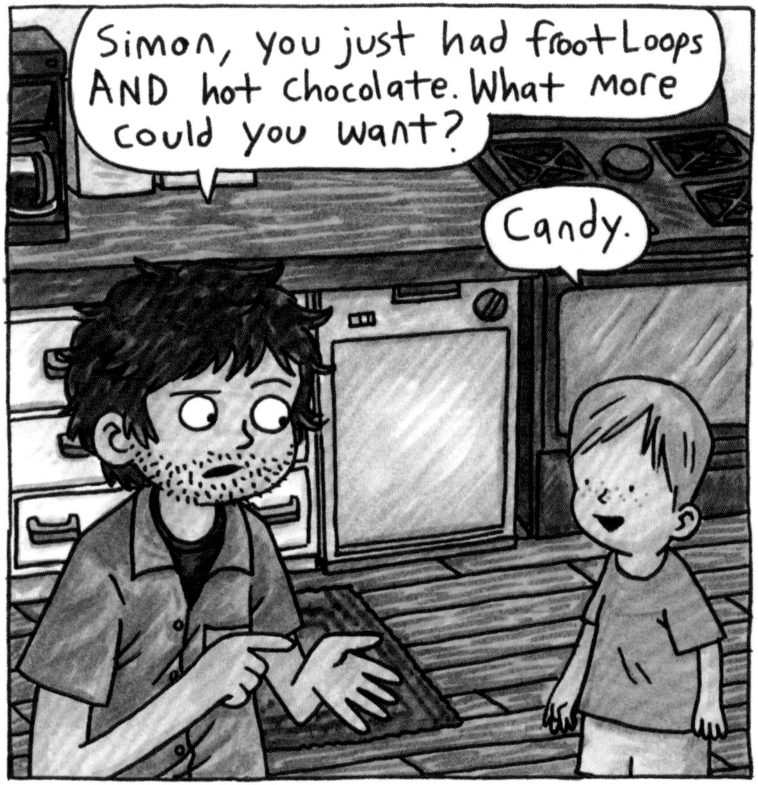
Simon, you just had froot Loops AND hot chocolate. What more could you want?
Candy.

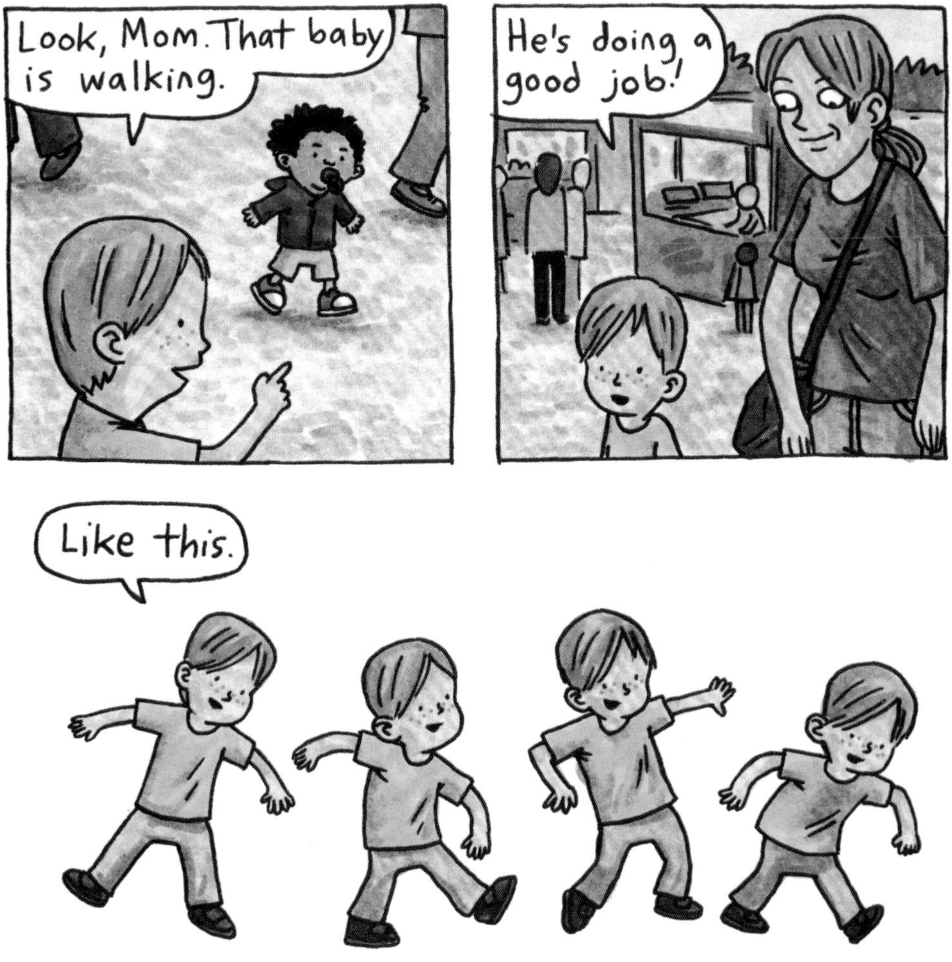
Look, Mom. That baby is walking.
He's doing a good job!
Like this.

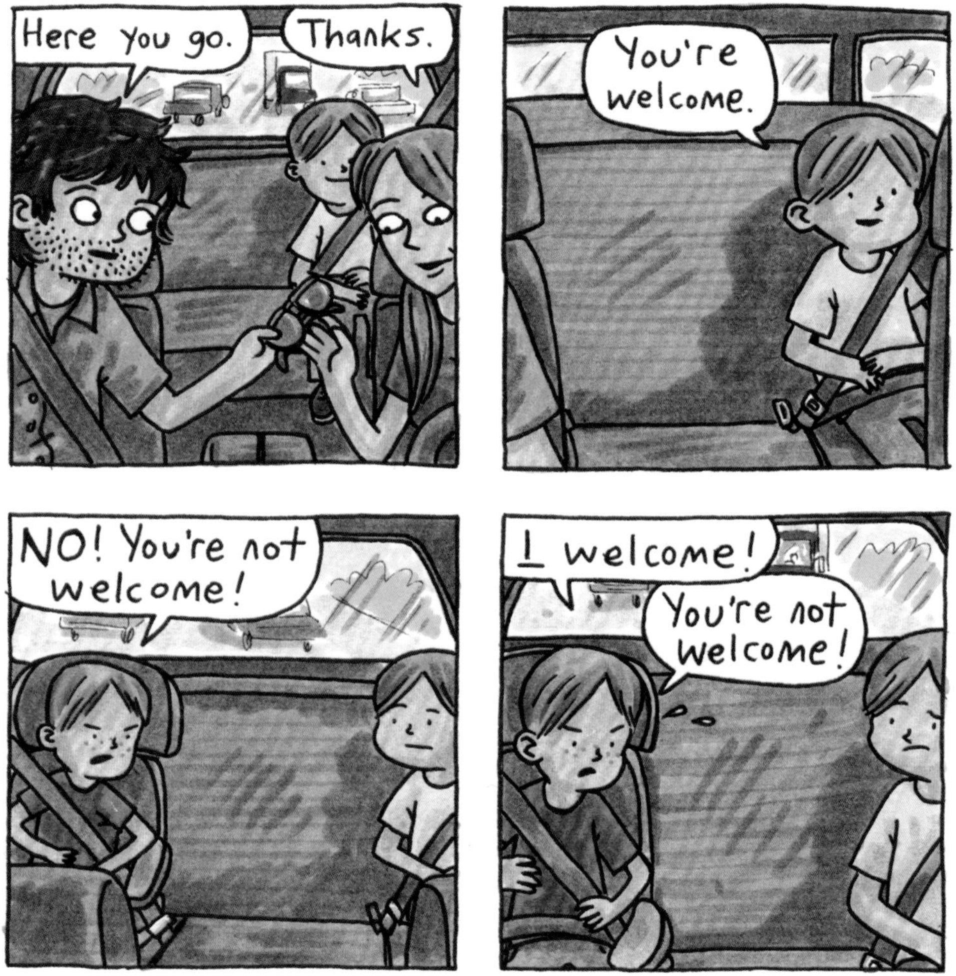
Here you go.
Thanks.
You're welcome.
NO! You're not welcome!
I welcome!
You're not welcome!

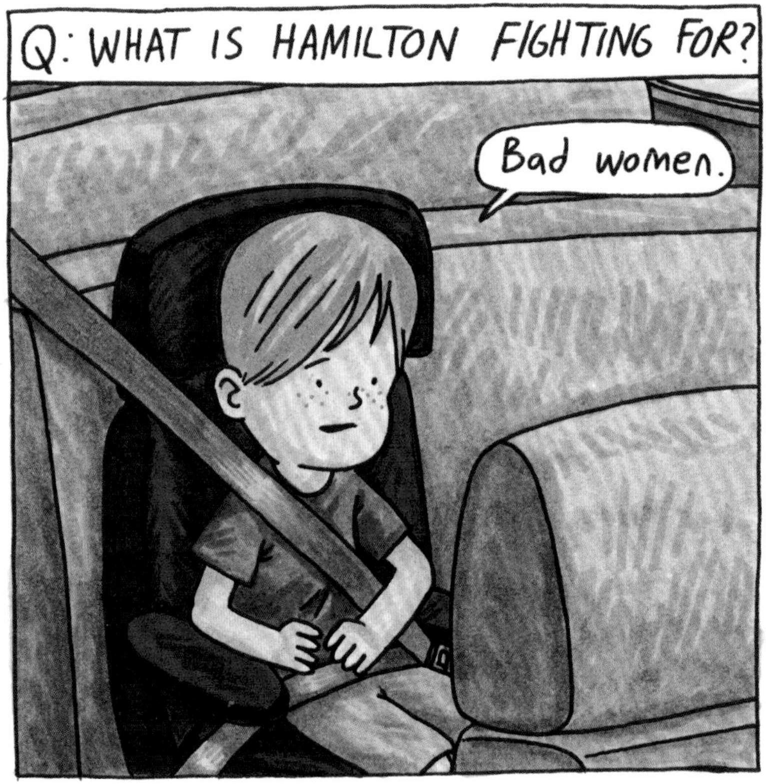
Q: WHAT IS HAMILTON FIGHTING FOR?
Bad women.

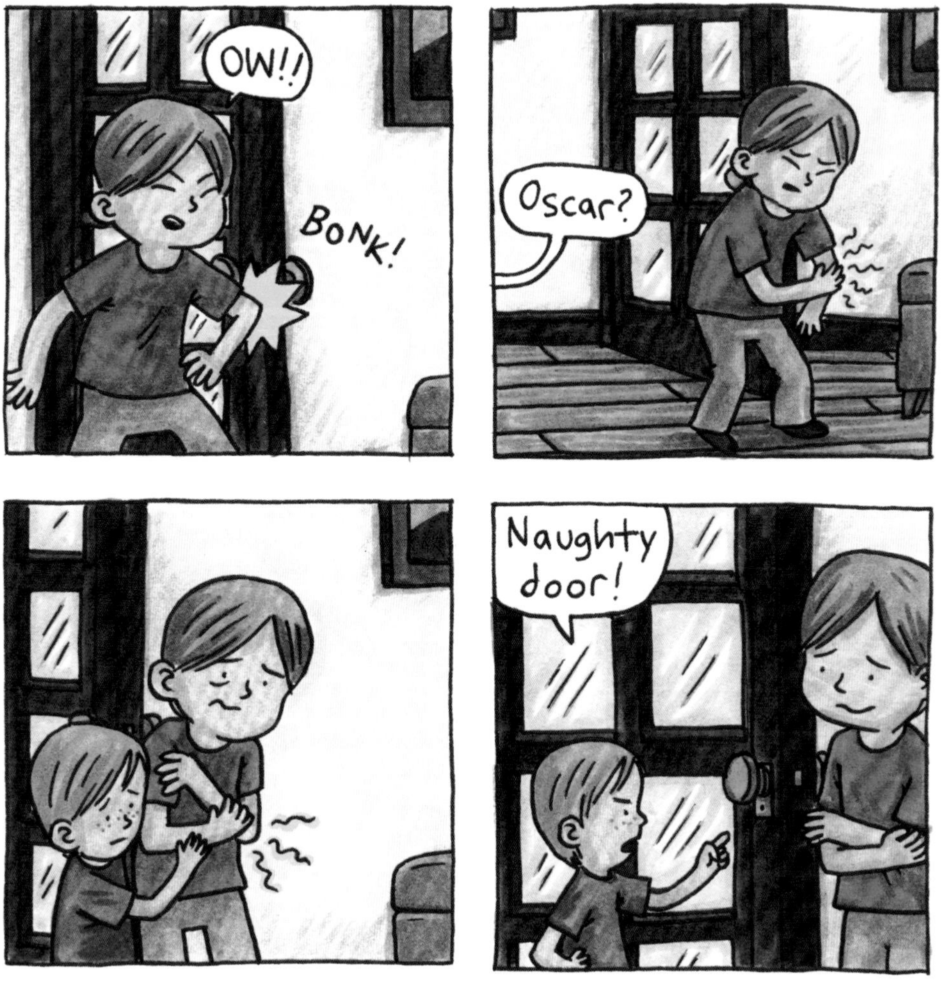
OW!!
BONK!
Oscar?
Naughty door!

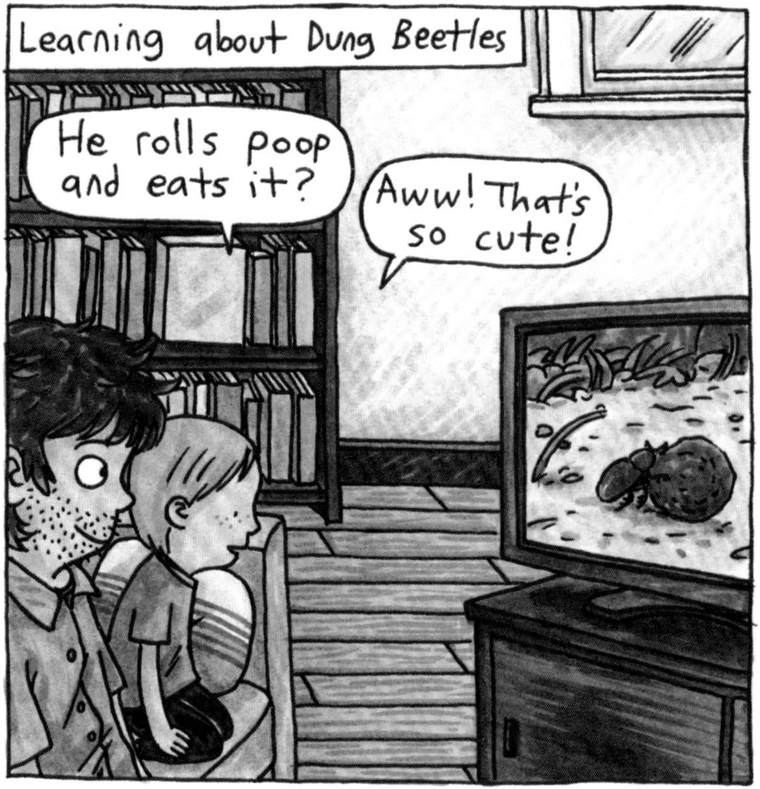
Learning about Dung Beetles
He rolls poop and eats it?
Aww! That's so cute!

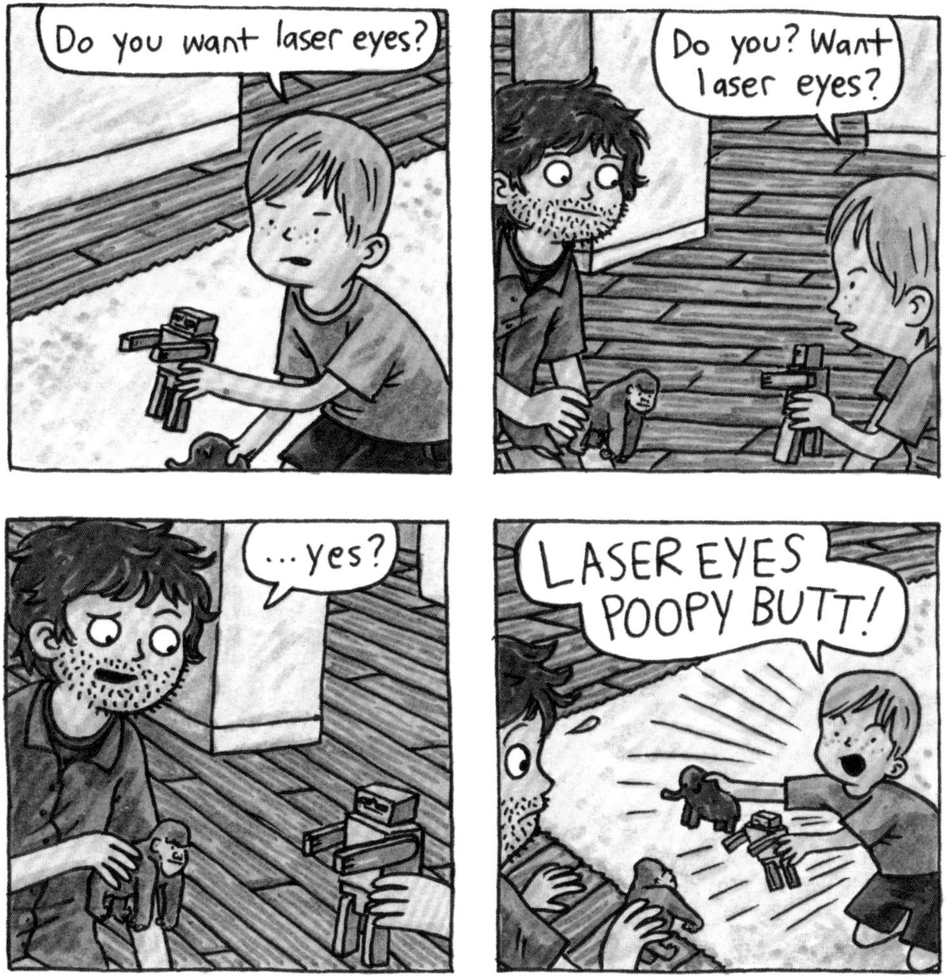
Do you want laser eyes?
Do you? Want laser eyes?
...yes?
LASER EYES POOPY BUTT!

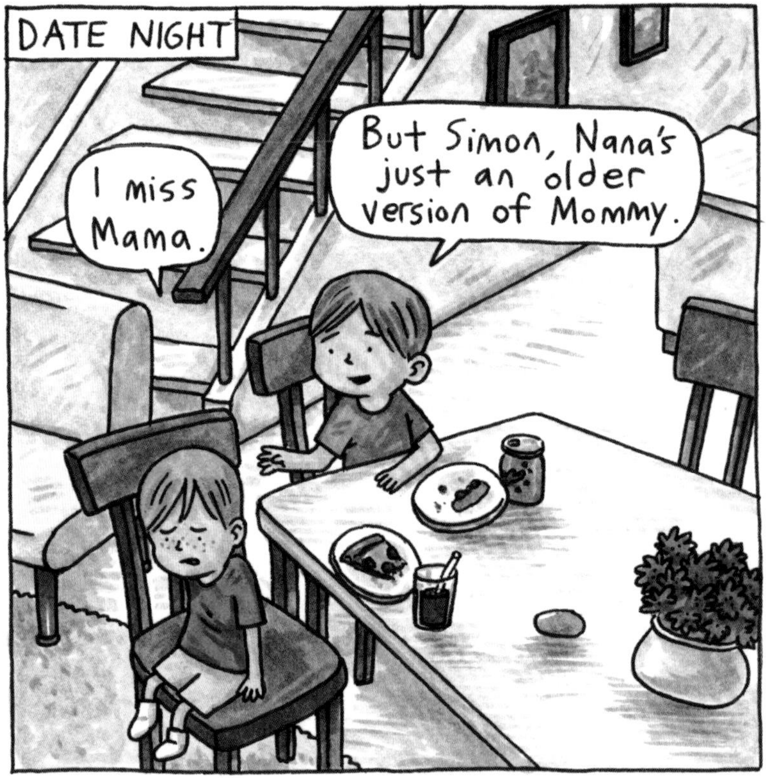
DATE NIGHT
I miss Mama.
But Simon, Nana's just an older version of Mommy.

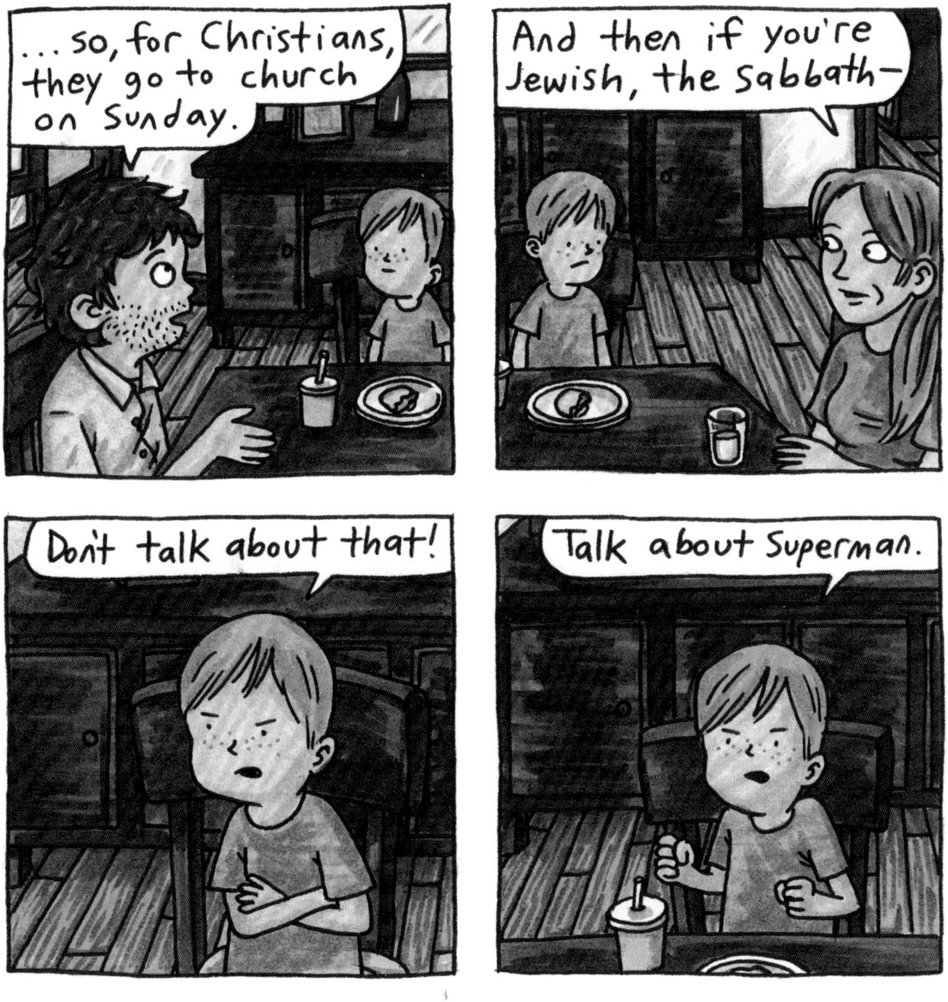
...so, for Christians, they go to church on Sunday.
And then if you're Jewish, the Sabbath—
Don't talk about that!
Talk about Superman.

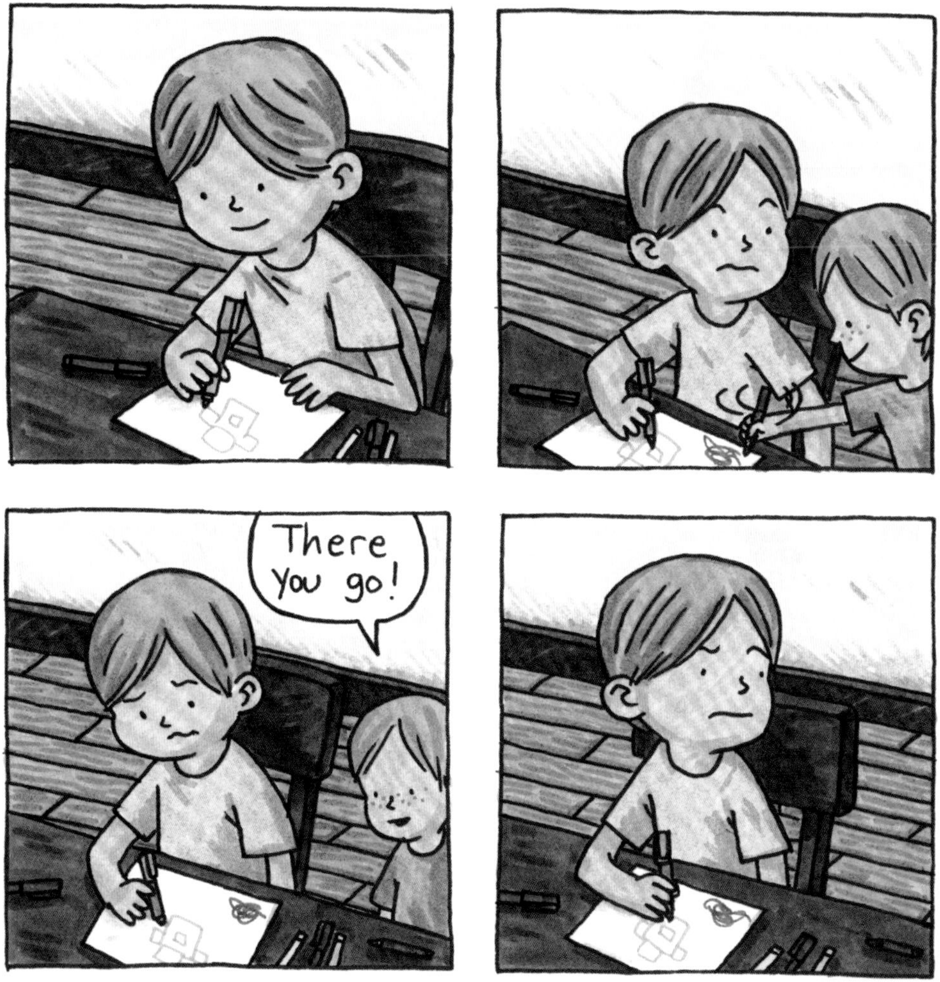
There you go!

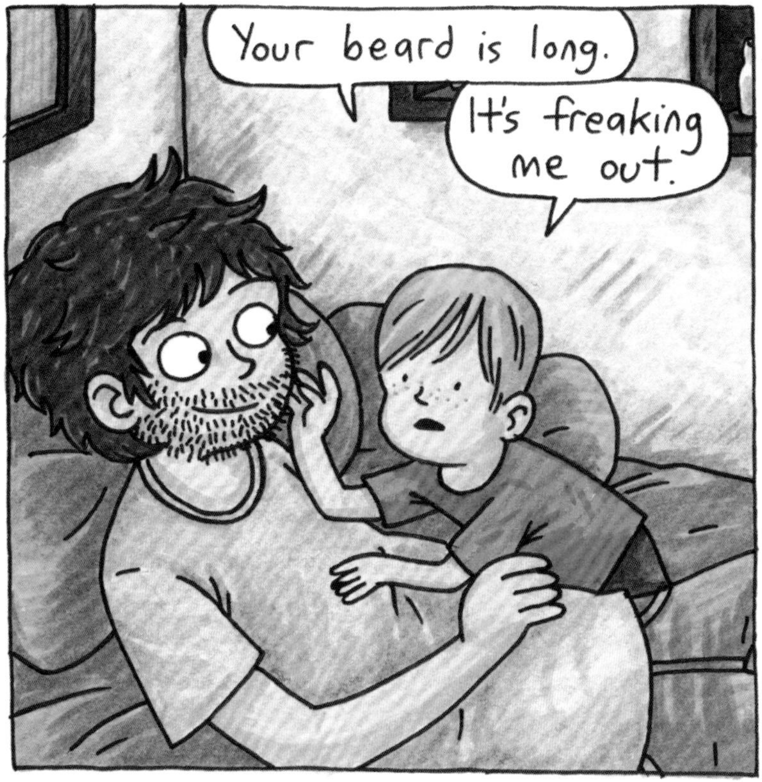
Your beard is long.
It's freaking me out.

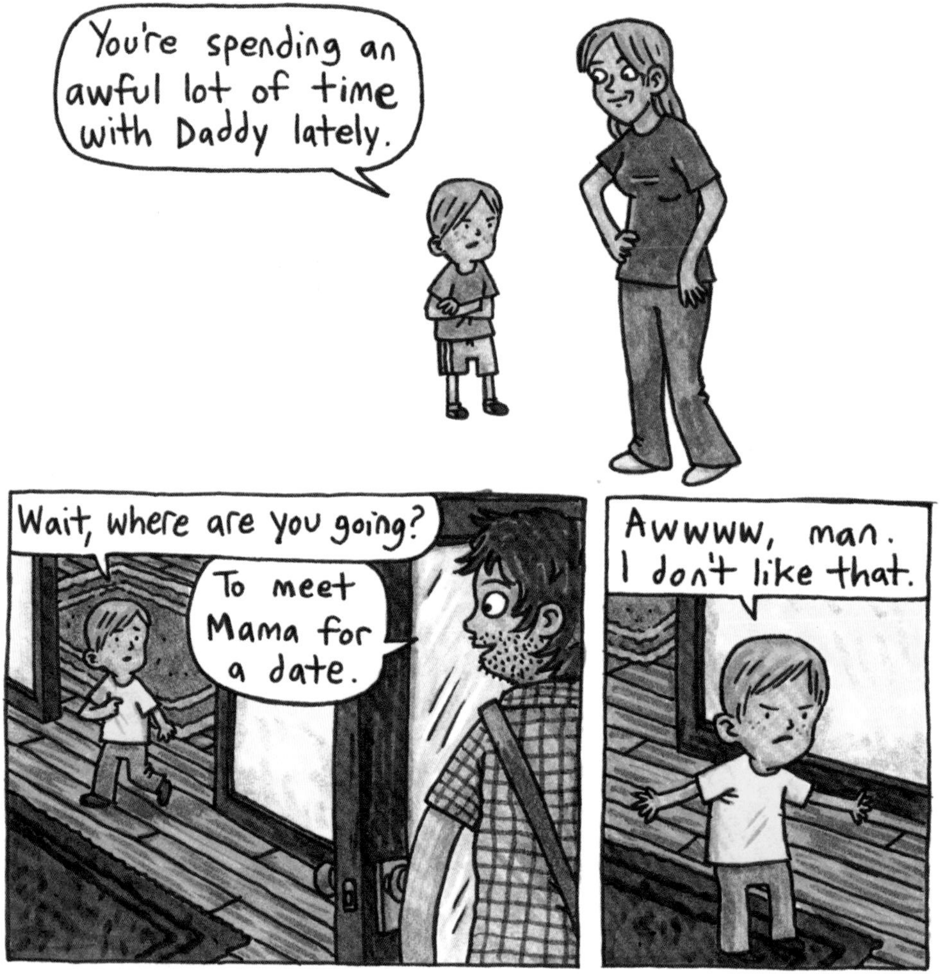

You're spending an awful lot of time with Daddy lately.
Wait, where are you going?
To meet Mama for a date.
Awwww, man. I don't like that.

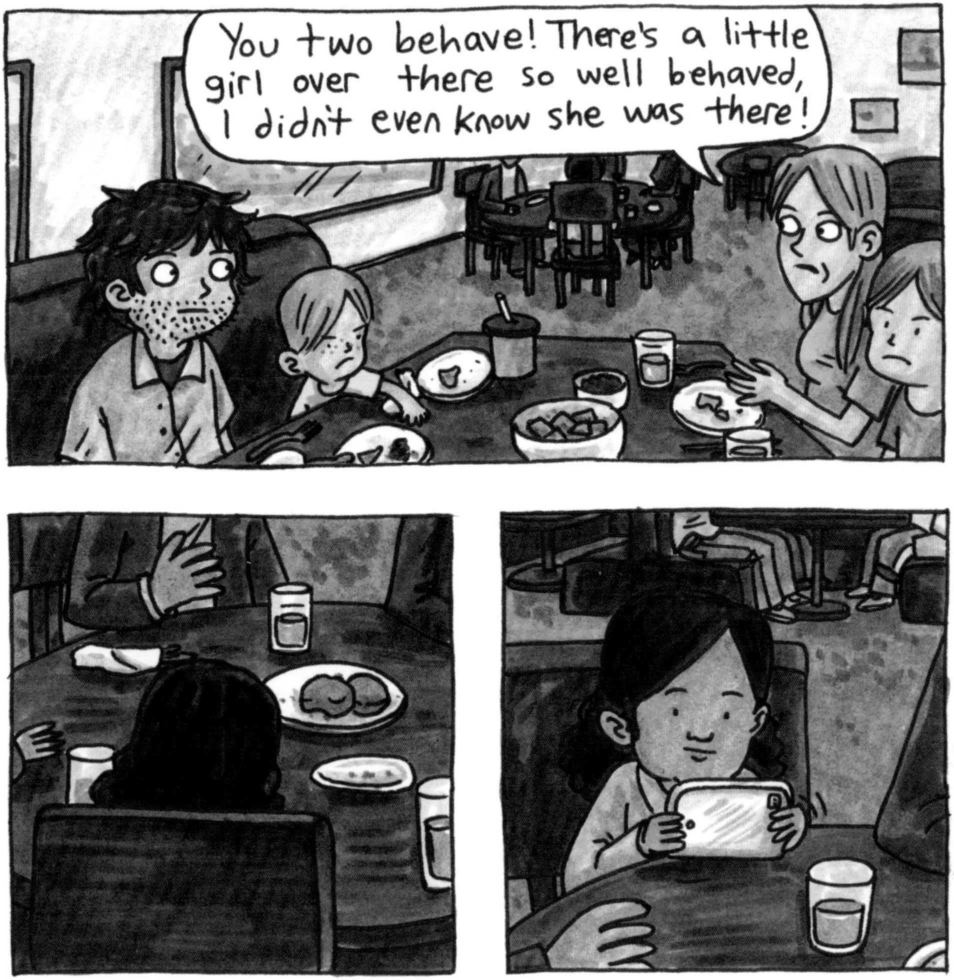
You two behave! There's a little girl over there so well behaved, I didn't even know she was there!

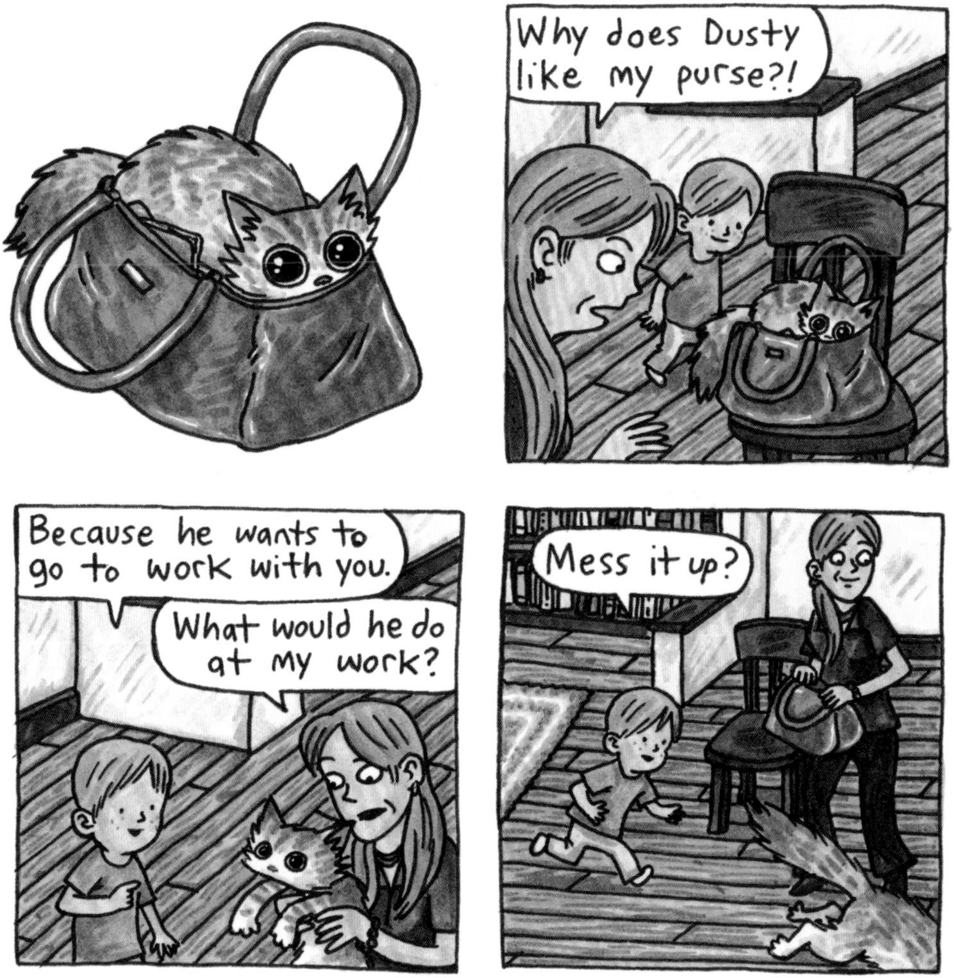
Why does Dusty like my purse?!
Because he wants to go to work with you.
What would he do at my work?
Mess it up?

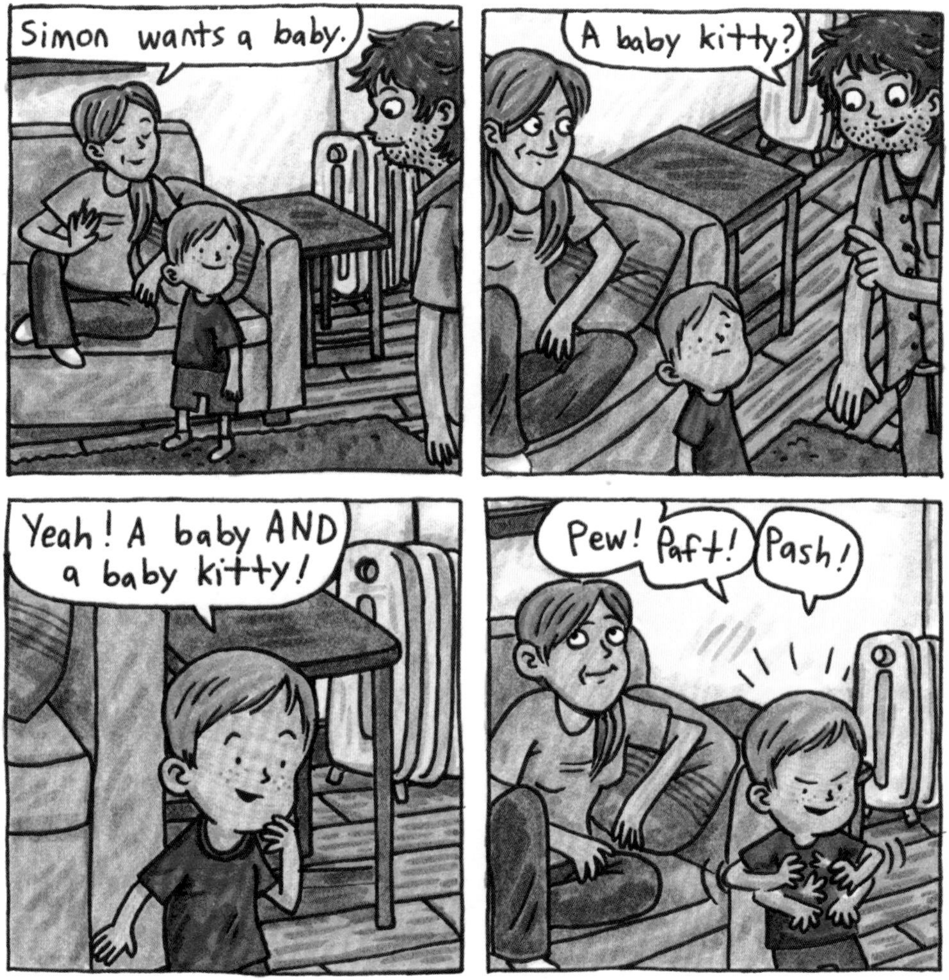
Simon wants a baby.
A baby kitty?
Yeah! A baby AND a baby kitty!
Pew!
Paft!
Pash!

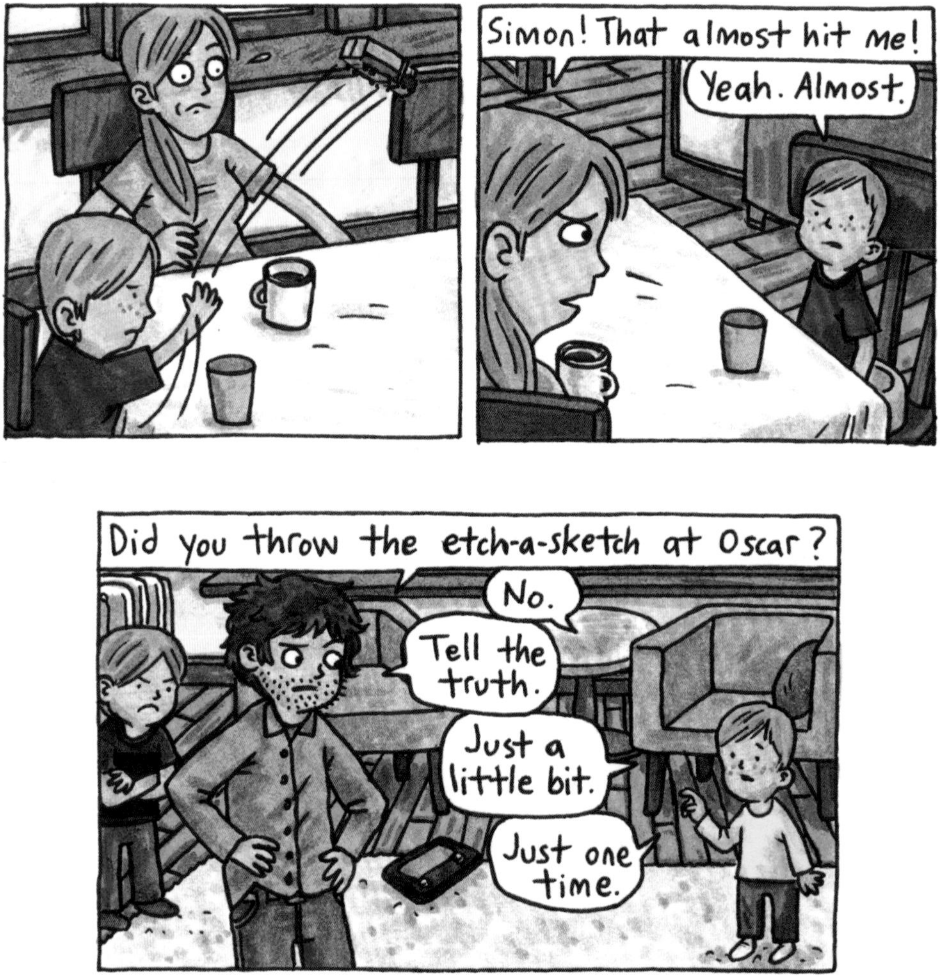
Simon! That almost hit me!
Yeah. Almost.
Did you throw the etch-a-sketch at Oscar?
No.
Tell the truth.
Just a little bit.
Just one time.

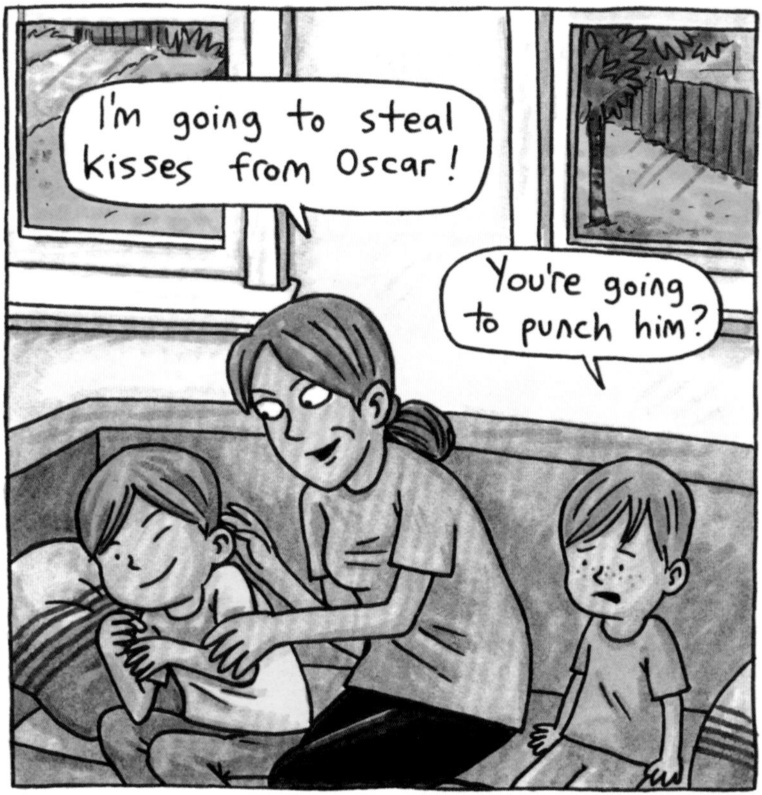
I'm going to steal kisses from Oscar!
You're going to punch him?

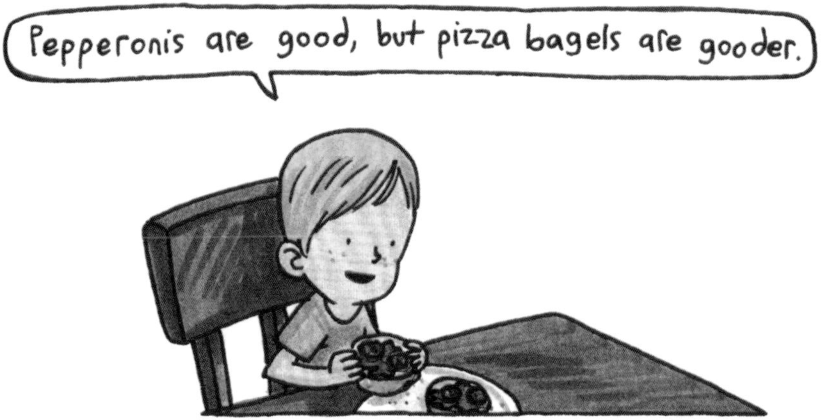
Pepperonis are good, but pizza bagels are gooder.

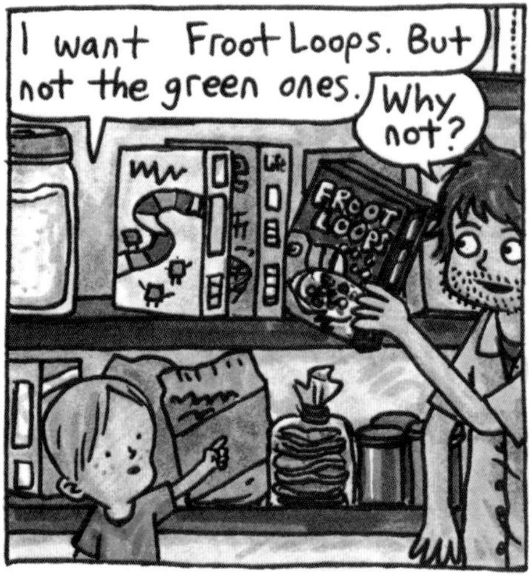
I want Froot Loops. But not the green ones.
Why not?
FROOT LOOPS

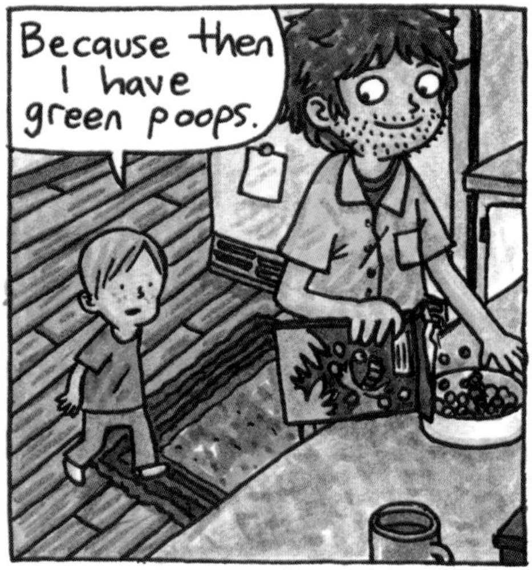
Because then I have green poops.

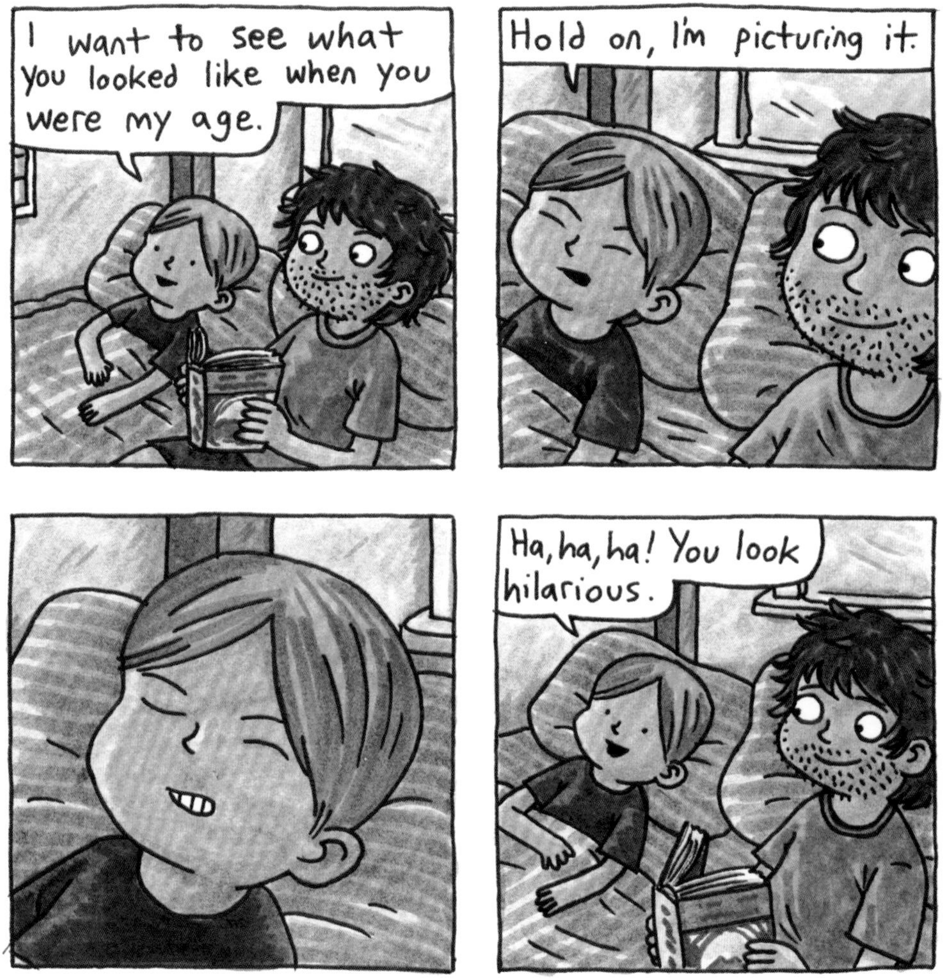
I want to see what you looked like when you were my age.
Hold on, I'm picturing it.
Ha, ha, ha! You look hilarious.

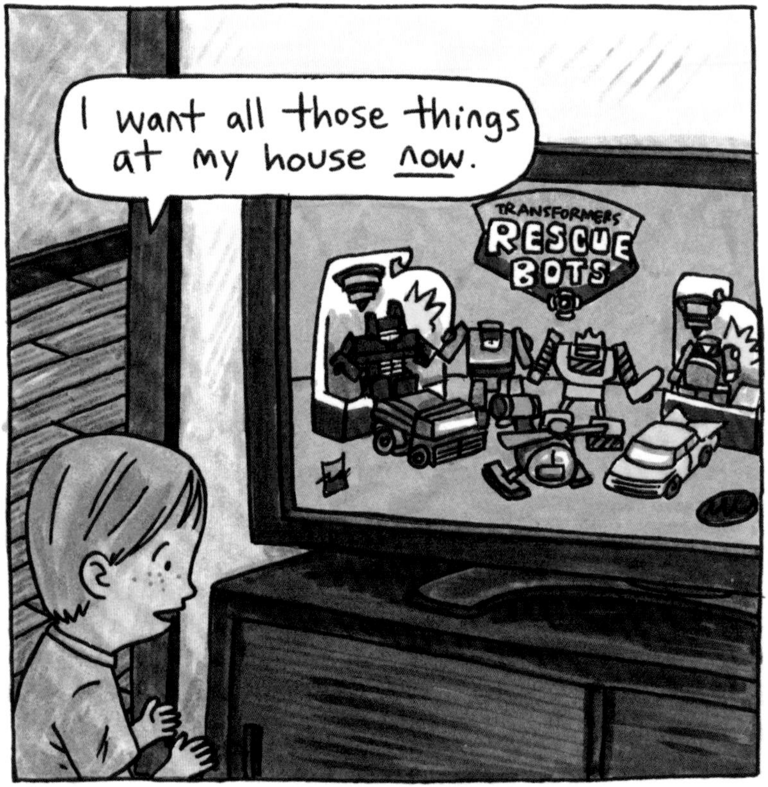
I want all those things at my house now.
TRANSFORMERS
RESCUE BOTS

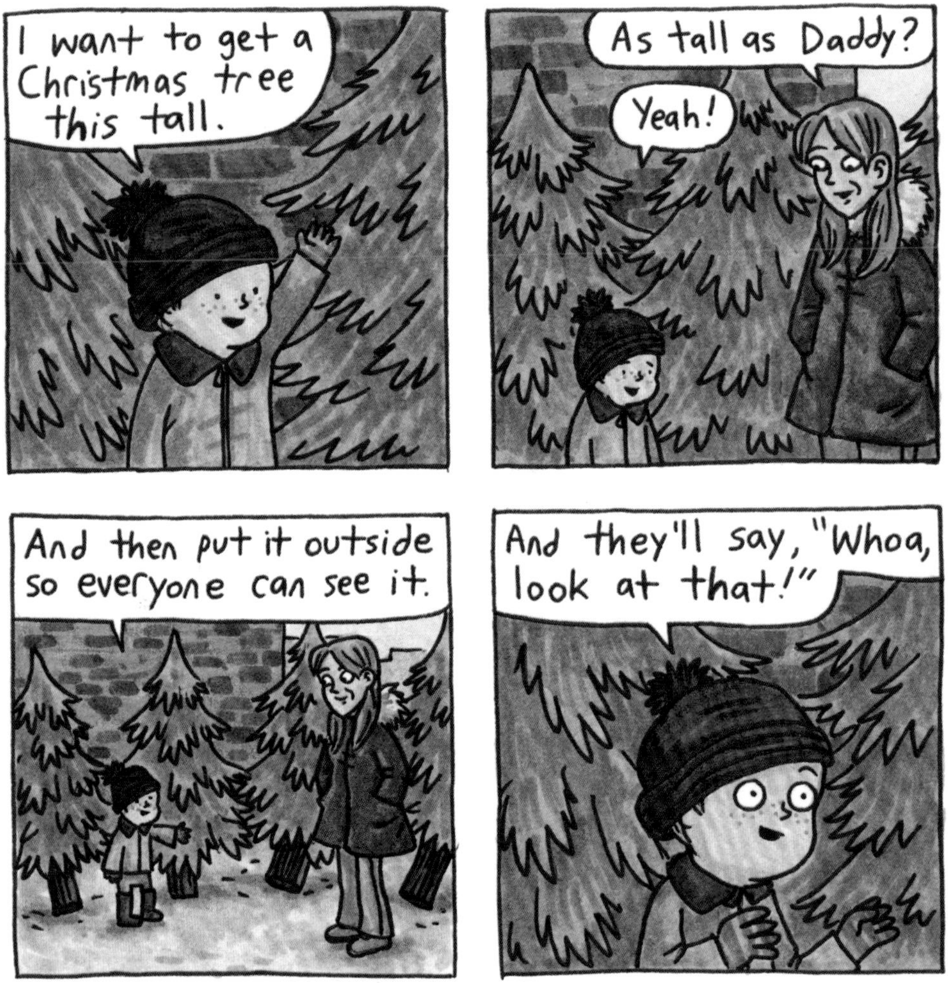
I want to get a Christmas tree this tall.
As tall as Daddy?
Yeah!
And then put it outside so everyone can see it.
And they'll say, "Whoa, look at that!"

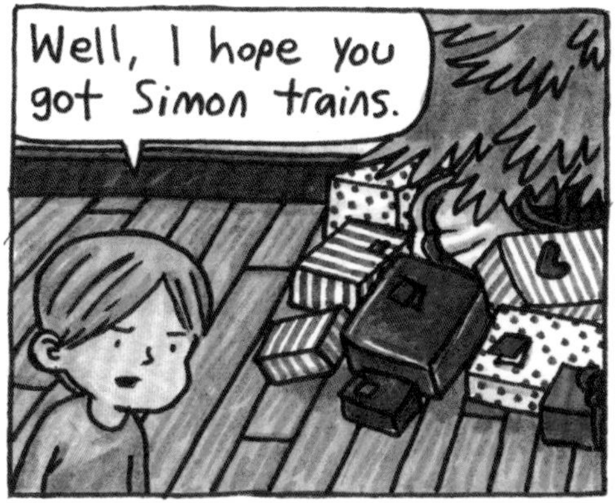
Well, I hope you got Simon trains.

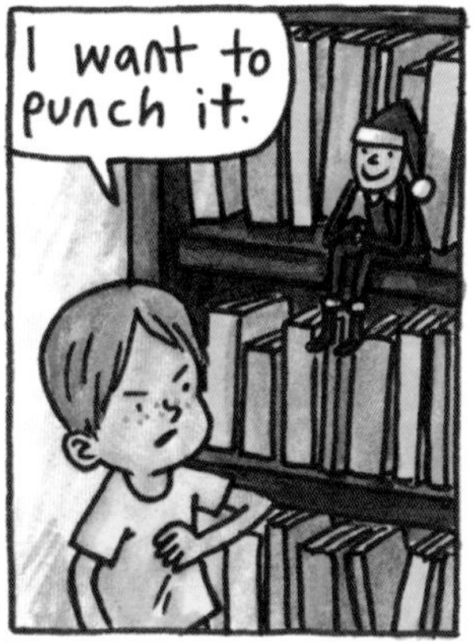
I want to punch it.

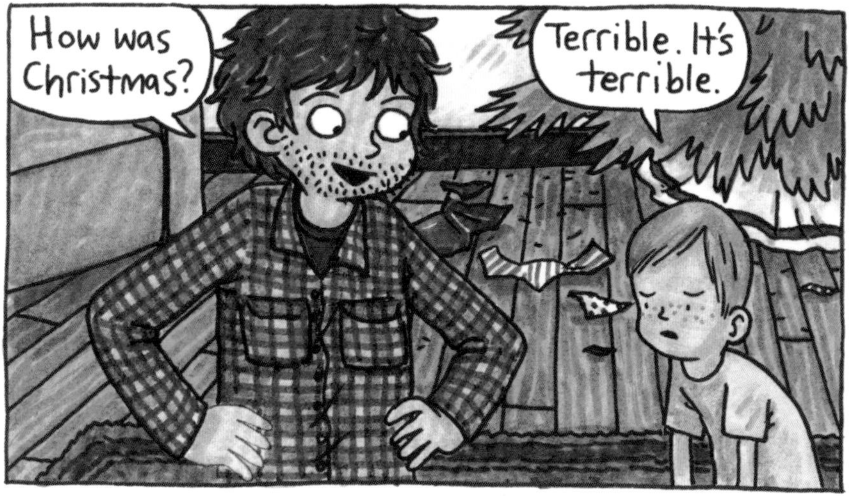
How was Christmas?
Terrible. It's terrible.

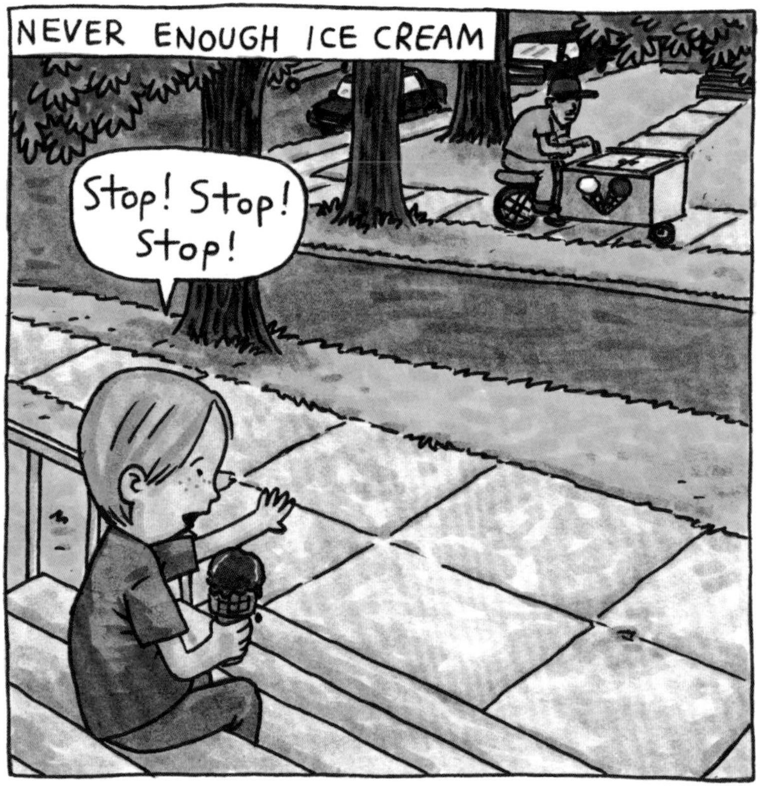
NEVER ENOUGH ICE CREAM
Stop! Stop! Stop!

There!
What does it mean?

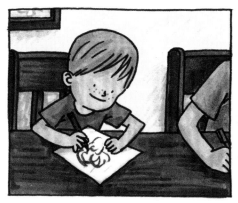

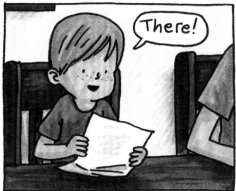

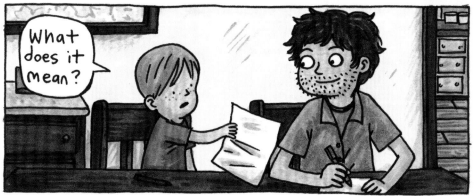

Do you know this one?
Hee! Hee! Ha! Ha!
Tickle Tickle
Tickle Tickle
Do you know this one?
You're going to hate it.

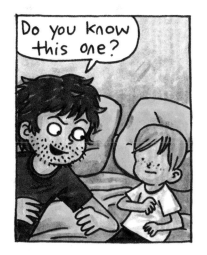

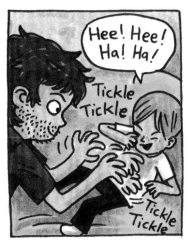

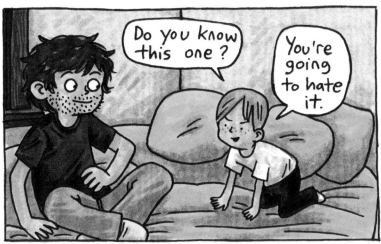

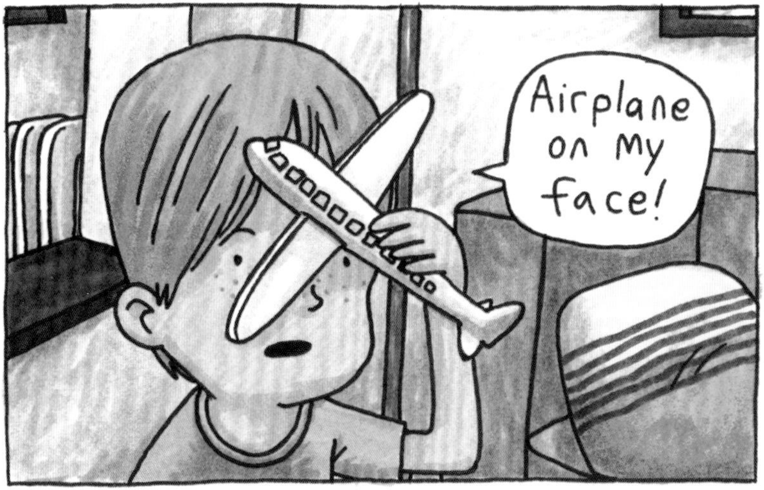
Airplane on my face!

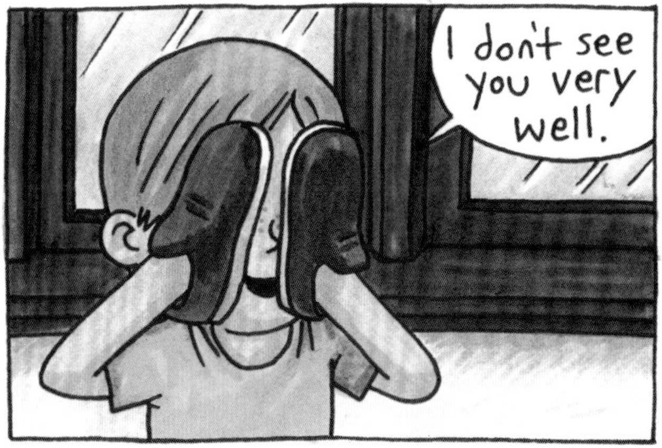
I don't see you very well.

Simon, why is your underwear on backwards?
Because I don't want to put my hand in the pocket.

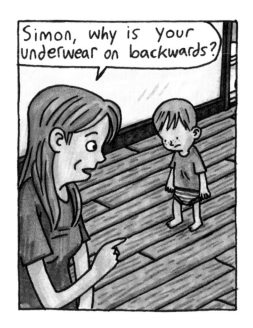

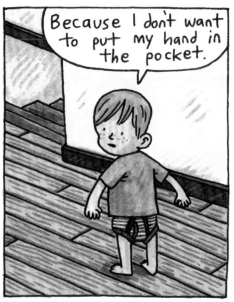

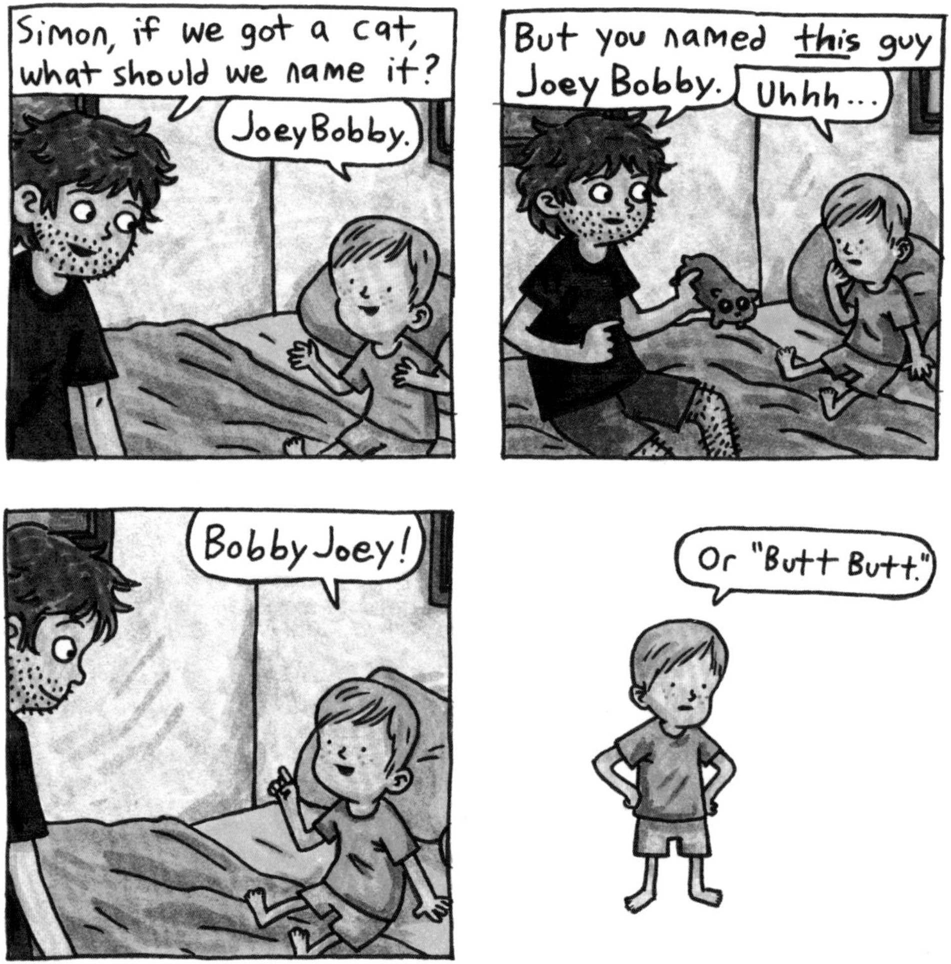
Simon, if we got a cat, what should we name it?
JoeyBobby.
But you named this guy Joey Bobby.
Uhhh...
BobbyJoey!
Or "Butt Butt."

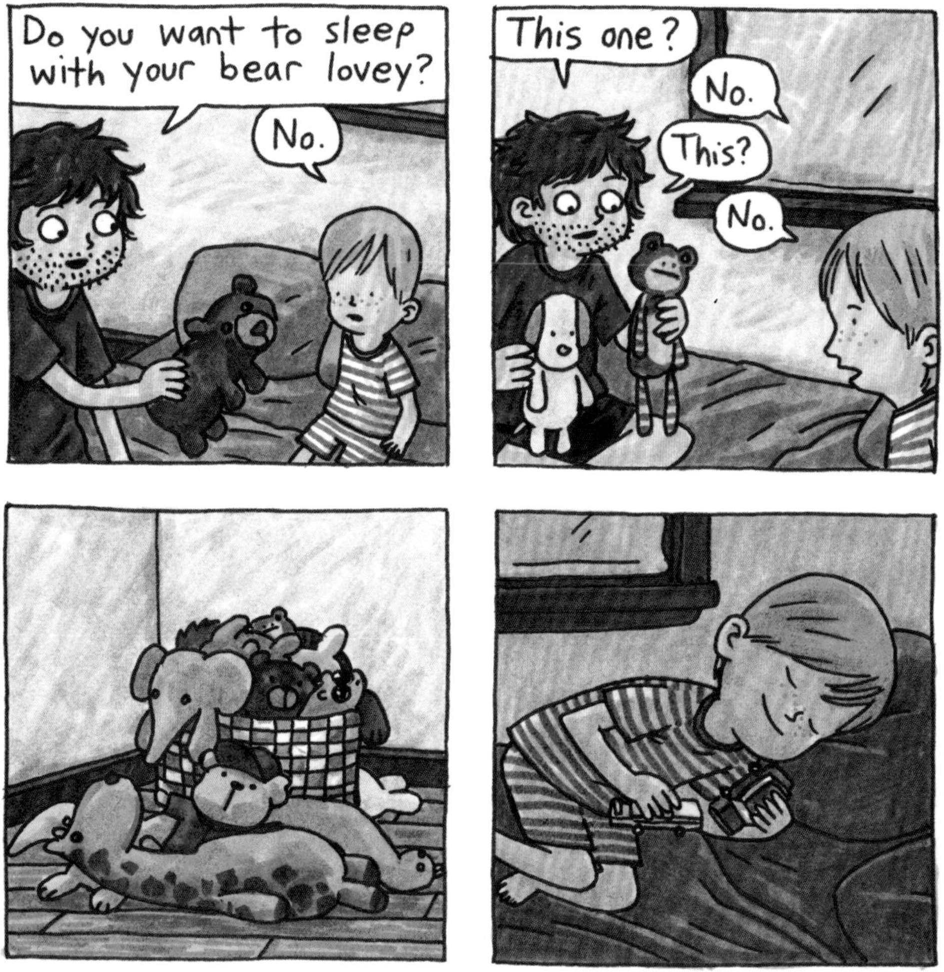
Do you want to sleep with your bear lovey?
No.
This one?
No.
This?
No.

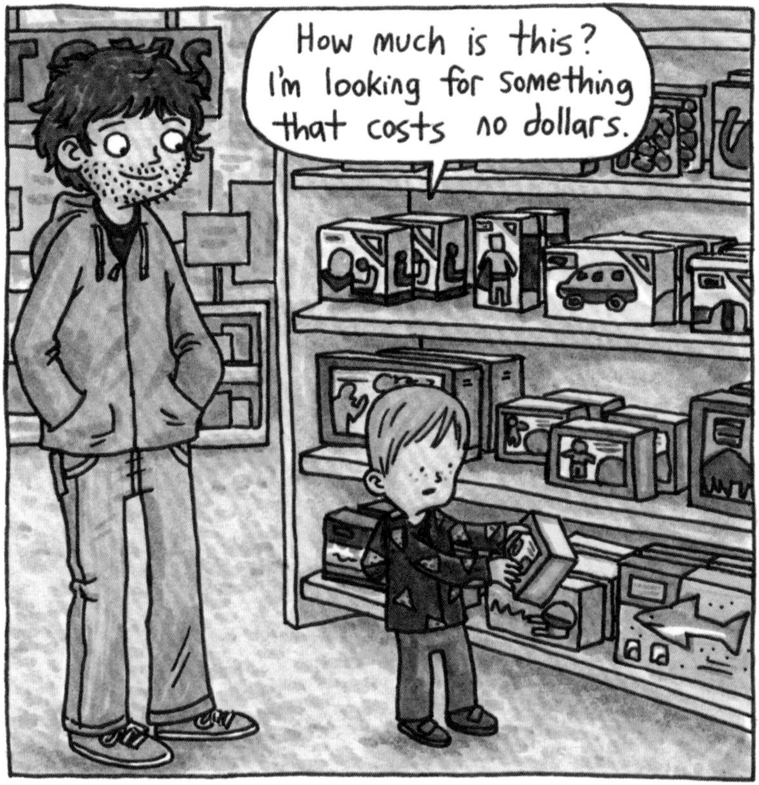
How much is this? I'm looking for something that costs no dollars.

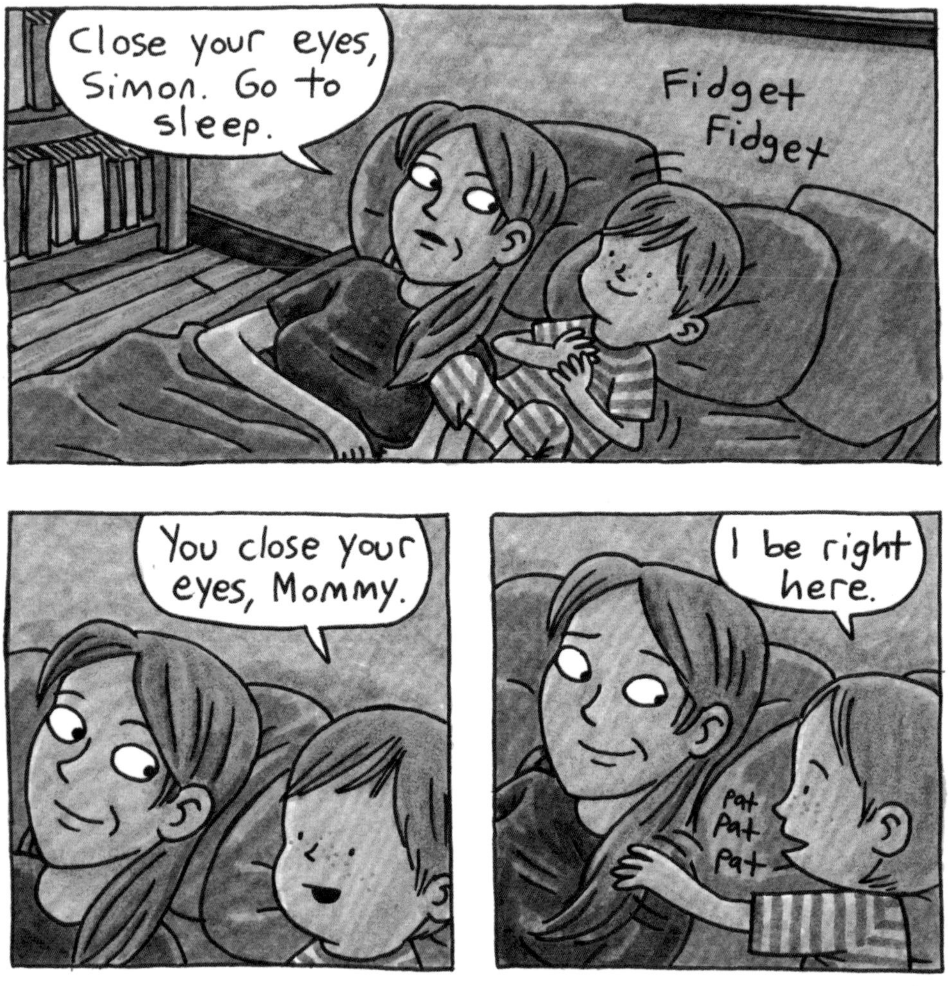
Close your eyes, Simon. Go to sleep.
Fidget Fidget
You close your eyes, Mommy.
I be right here.
pat pat pat

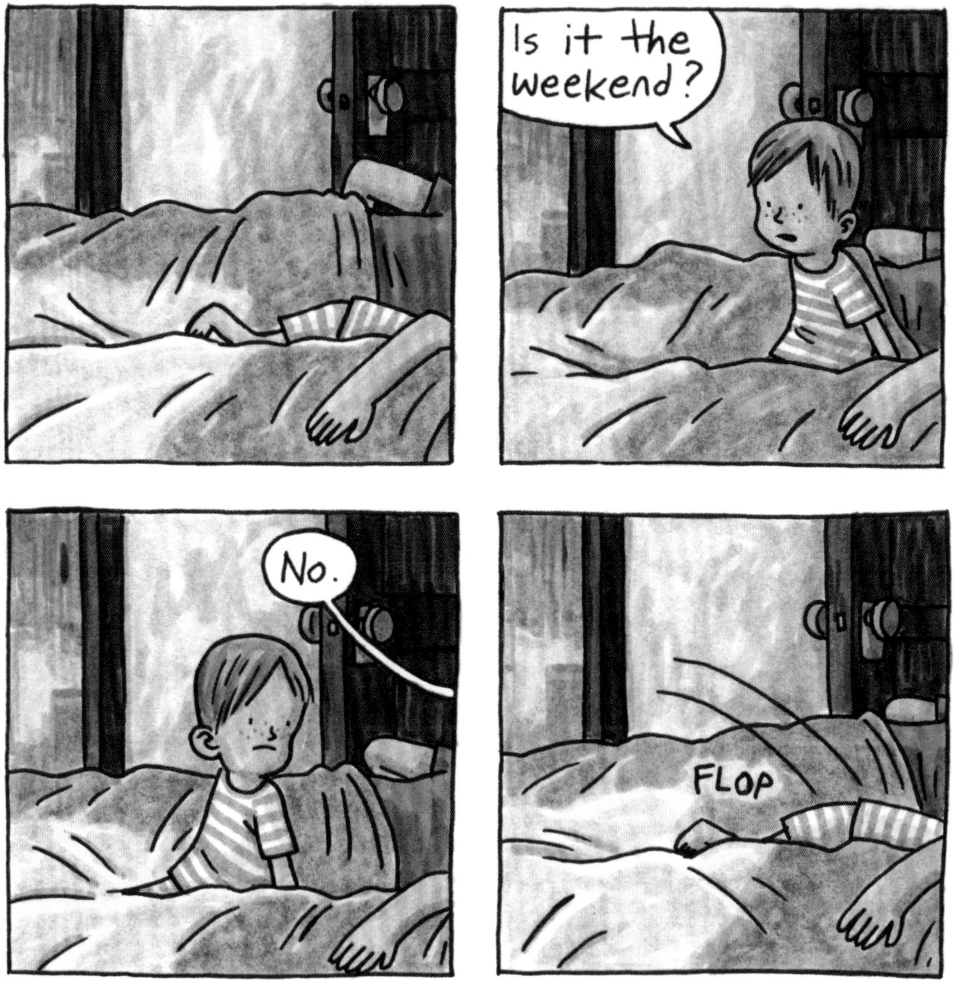
Is it the weekend?
No.
FLOP

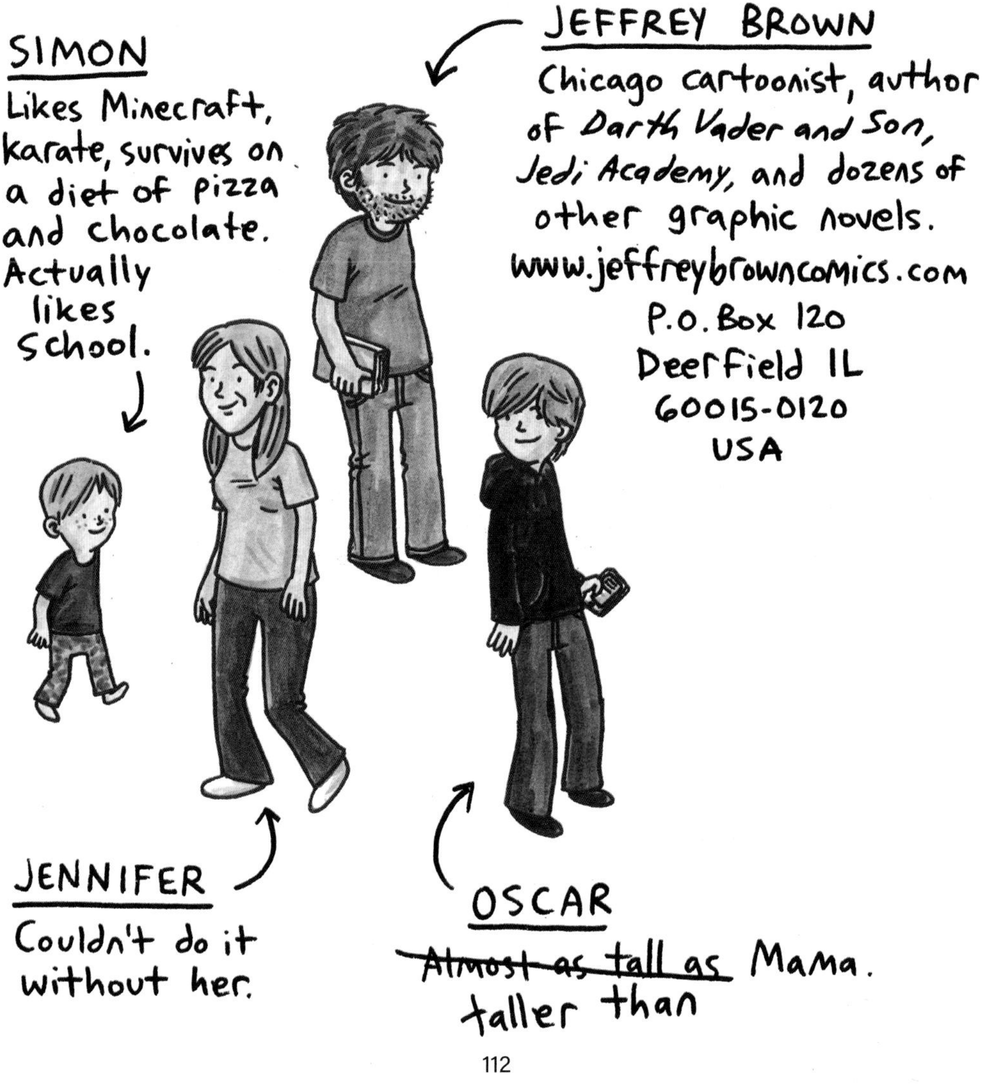
SIMON
Likes Minecraft, karate, survives on a diet of pizza and chocolate. Actually likes school.
JEFFREY BROWN
Chicago cartoonist, author of *Darth Vader and Son*, *Jedi Academy*, and dozens of other graphic novels.
www.jeffreybrowncomics.com
P.O. Box 120
Deerfield IL
60015-0120
USA
JENNIFER
Couldn't do it without her.
OSCAR
~~Almost as tall as~~ Mama.
taller than